Teacher and Paraprofessional
Work Productivity

Teacher and Paraprofessional Work Productivity

A Public School Cost Effectiveness Study

Eaton H. Conant
University of Oregon

Lexington Books
D.C. Heath and Company
Lexington, Massachusetts
Toronto   London

Library of Congress Cataloging in Publication Data

Conant, Eaton H.
   Teacher and paraprofessional work productivity.

   1. Schools—Portland, Or.—Accounting. 2. Portland School District—
Statistics. I. Title.
LB2826.5.P67C66   379'.157   73-9915
ISBN 0-669-86991-0

Published simultaneously in Canada.

Printed in the United States of America.

International Standard Book Number: 0-669-86991-0

Library of Congress Catalog Card Number: 73-9915

To Beth, and Jim, Kate, Clarke, and Keith

Contents

List of Tables

Preface

Since the middle 1960s, public school districts in the nation have added thousands of paraprofessionals to their employment roles in a manpower staffing innovation that has important implications for students, school staff, and taxpayers. A consequence of these trends for paraprofessional employment is that the traditional teaching division of labor in schools is being substantially changed to provide teachers with work assistance and opportunities to specialize more effectively in instructional tasks. The central questions examined in this study are: Has the new teacher-paraprofessional division of school work fundamentally changed the kinds and amounts of instruction that are performed in the schools, and can the costs of this new work division be justified in terms of student learning experiences and other benefits it may confer?

The research required exceptional cooperation from many members of the staff of School District Number One of Portland, Oregon. Over one hundred teachers and paraprofessionals who must remain nameless assisted by cooperating in the empirical studies essential to the research. Members of the district administrative staff spent many hours with us discussing elements of the project. Mr. Charles Clemans, Dr. James Holmes, and Dr. George Ingebo especially deserve thanks for their generous assistance. Other district staff members too numerous to mention also provided valuable assistance. A most rewarding experience for us was to get to know the high quality of persons to be found in this large city district.

Many colleagues and research assistants at the University of Oregon provided valuable assistance. Industrial Relations Institute Research Assistants Roger Bannister, Jan Bisschop, Johan DeVoogd, Al Hallberg, Cheedle Millard, Don Rice, and Robert Shelton participated in the work studies or data analyses. Professor James Bruno of the University of California at Los Angeles was unusually generous with counsel and advice.

This was an extensive research effort for a principal investigator to undertake. The complete study consists of related substudies of staff work, cost and modeling analyses, and test score analysis, each of which was a major study in itself. At the initiation of the project, we did not know if extensive work observations, detailed cost data, and useful student test score results could be obtained in a large school district. And few previous investigators had tried to apply systems analysis methods to work and cost data of the kind we required. The project could not have met the challenges involved in obtaining and analyzing the necessary information without the generous assistance of all the persons named above.

Grateful thanks are due to all these persons. Of course, errors and omissions are the sole responsibility of the principal researcher and author.

Eaton H. Conant

University of Oregon

Acknowledgments

The research analysis reported herein was performed with support from a manpower institutional grant from the U.S. Department of Labor to the Industrial Relations Institute, University of Oregon. Field research for the study was supported by a grant from the U.S. Office of Education. Contractors undertaking such projects under Government sponsorship are encouraged to express freely their professional judgment in the conduct of the project. Points of view or opinions stated do not, therefore, necessarily represent official positions or policy of any government agency.

Teacher and Paraprofessional
Work Productivity

1

The New Division of Work in the Schools

Two major developments in recent years have caused a change in the nature of employment in public education. One of these developments, which has been much discussed elsewhere, is the emergence of collective bargaining in school employment relations. A second important change has not until now been systematically discussed. This development is a new effort by educational administrators to change traditional teacher assignment and work methods in order to derive greater instructional productivity from the teaching staff, including new schemes for team teaching, specialization in teaching subject matter, and other innovations that alter customary work methods and affect the traditional organization of teaching employment.

The most extensive change educational managers have made in order to increase teaching effectiveness has been the employment of teaching paraprofessionals in the schools. Customary methods of assigning teachers to classes and work are now widely modified, especially in lower grades, by new systems that assign paraprofessional assistants to teach and assist teachers in the school division of labor. Since the 1960s, most major school districts and many smaller ones have added thousands of nonprofessionals to their employment rolls in the most extensive change in educational manpower practices in decades.

For years the public schools have employed teachers in work roles where, especially at lower grade levels, teachers have been generalists who teach multiple subjects and function as classroom wardens and monitors of an annual cohort of students. Where specialization is achieved at all, it is usually by subject matter and grade level of courses taught. Even then, teachers perform many other functions in the schools in addition to instruction. This work role—part teacher, part child warden, and part housekeeper—is a venerable one that educational administrators have attempted to change by introducing paraprofessional aides into the classroom. Labor and manpower specialists would recognize this employment change as an effort to improve labor efficiency by introducing greater specialization and extending the division of labor in the schools.

The history of development of professions indicates professional work efficiency is increased and more quality work is done when professions increase specialization in their division of labor. Specialization in the professions is achieved in one of several ways. One of these ways is for less than professional trained personnel to assume the more nonprofessional and routine tasks of professionals. The efficiency gains that may result are realized for several reasons. Less costly nonprofessional labor is substituted for more costly

1

professional labor to do the less demanding work. At the same time, professionals are freed to apply their specialized and more expensive talents to more important tasks.

Several of the professions are well advanced in making application of these principles of specialization. In the medical arts, the employment of various levels of medical assistants has developed so substantially in the last two decades that paramedical assistants are now regarded as conventional. However, in education the situation is not so far advanced. Only in the past decade, have several factors combined to stimulate school administrators to modify work patterns.

One of the most important of these stimuli is the general view, in education circles, that conventional work assignment patterns for teachers are unsatisfactory to teachers, wasteful of their valuable work time, and not very defensible in terms of the educational achievement they produce in children. Internal and external criticisms about these deficiencies in conventional teaching methods have been major incentives in spurring administrators to employ nonprofessionals and modify the division of instructional labor.

One finds in the literature of education, for example, a large body of discussion which is occupied with criticism of existing assignment patterns in the traditional, single teacher in classroom, division of labor. The authors of this criticism include both teachers and administrators. Their principal complaint about teacher work is that work is so overburdened with noninstructional and nonprofessional routine tasks that teachers do not have sufficient time to teach. Before this study was performed, there were no studies available that could confirm or refute this complaint. However, the pervasiveness of the complaints indicates that real deficiencies were one basis for efforts to alter work practices.

Federal programs in assistance to education, especially compensatory education for minority disadvantaged children, have also stimulated employment of paraprofessionals in recent years. These programs have had the purpose of encouraging local school districts to improve education for poor and minority children and have provided extra resources for teaching manpower for that purpose. To the extent that compensatory education directors equated educational improvement with more intensive instruction and reduced teacher-pupil ratios, these directors tended to view new teacher paraprofessional work systems as means for more intensive instruction. And because federal grants carried provisions that local nonprofessionals should be employed in compensatory programs, nonprofessional employment in schools was further stimulated.

It is doubtful, however, if decisions to employ paraprofessionals in educational systems would have been made by employers if facilitating changes in the ratios of teacher and unskilled labor earnings had not developed in the economy in recent years. Reviews of any of the historical wage and earnings chronologies available in census and other government sources show that throughout the 1930s and most of the 1940s, the average annual earnings of public school teachers in the nation were nearly equal to the average annual earnings of unskilled workers. In the 1950s and throughout the period to the mid 1960s, teacher annual earnings made gradual but substantial relative improvement in comparison to unskilled worker earnings. By the mid 1960s, average teacher earnings had improved to near equality with the annual average for skilled workers in the economy and were several thousand dollars above levels for unskilled workers.

The implication of these changes is that until the 60s teacher labor could be purchased at levels of costs comparable to levels for unskilled labor, and there was no incentive for employers to consider specialization of the teaching division of labor and substitution of unskilled labor for teacher labor. Only after teachers achieved a skilled labor cost differential in the 60s were potential cost savings advantages available. Employer pursuit of this advantage has also been facilitated by the abundant labor supply of secondary labor force women in less skilled categories that surveys have identified during these years. This network of broader economic relationships has provided incentives and opportunities for educational employers to use less skilled paraprofessional labor commencing in the 60s. In addition, more particular economic pressures have operated within this larger framework to stimulate employers to modify the traditional teaching division of labor.

Educational managers are required to acknowledge the fact that theirs is a labor-intensive service industry where labor costs of instruction are typically in excess of 70 percent of the total costs represented in annual operating budgets. The magnitude of labor costs as a proportion of all operating costs has forced managers to be very sensitive to changes in teacher salary costs. For some time now, administrators have faced the dilemma that special groups have demanded more effective educational services, even while voters in general have frequently refused to vote affirmatively for budget increases. Voter failures to approve budgets have peaked in recent years, moreover, at the same time that more militant teachers have gained increased effectiveness in applying bargaining pressures to gain earnings raises. Because they have been placed in circumstances where labor costs have increased while public financial support has declined, administrators have had to consider basic alternatives to conventional methods of delivering instruction. One choice has been an instructional work system, utilizing professionals and paraprofessionals, that may deliver more effective instruction at reduced unit labor costs.

These are the reasons why school administrators have teamed teachers and paraprofessionals in the instruction process. However, no evidence has been available to indicate if this instructional system has achieved any economic or noneconomic advantages. The purpose of this study was to measure the work produced by teachers and paraprofessionals to determine if the new work division had productive instructional advantages. A related objective was to identify the economic costs and educational benefits that the teacher-paraprofessional teaming experienced and produced. The study is the first to examine the work of teachers and nonprofessionals at schools to comprehensively identify the nature of the work they perform in instructional and noninstructional duties. In addition, the economic efficiency of the new work system is appraised where the study compares costs of the new division of work with labor costs of traditional work methods. The study also evaluates the benefits produced by the introduction of paraprofessionals as it reviews the gains in educational achievement school children experienced before and after the new staffing system was installed.

The results of the study should be of interest to persons with diverse backgrounds who have reasons to be concerned about effective organization of teacher work, work productivity of teachers and paraprofessionals, and the economic costs and educational benefits of instruction. While the study is primarily a study of the economics of manpower utilization with a cost-effectiveness emphasis, the original information the study has produced about the nature of instructional work should be of interest to persons other than labor and manpower specialists. Moreover, while the details of the research focus on measuring labor outputs in education and cost-effectiveness results of education work systems, the results have implications for several private and public policy areas.

Concerning public policy and program implications, perhaps the most relevant programs are those with the objective of creating employment for disadvantaged persons as nonprofessionals in public sector institutions. The Congress has passed bills in the last several years to create public service opportunities for paraprofessional employment. However, there has been extensive debate within branches of the federal establishment about the efficacy of these efforts, with negative evaluations coming from persons who believe funding of paraprofessional positions reflects make-work practices for jobs the economy will not sustain when federal funding ceases. Proponents of nonprofessional employment for the poor argue, on the other hand, that there are abundant opportunities to redesign jobs or create new specialties in public work so the poor can find employment.

At the heart of arguments about public funding of paraprofessional jobs are assumptions about efficiency in work that opponents and proponents have seldom explicitly stated. Those who favor federal expenditures have argued that many existing public jobs are not efficiently specialized according to the value of their skill requirements and labor costs. They also assume that bureaucratic systems tend to exaggerate the hierarchical importance of job tasks with the result that there is distortion between job demands, hiring requirements, and compensation systems that could not exist in competitive, private markets.

For their part, opponents of public paraprofessional employment plans find it difficult to believe that less than "fully qualified" persons will perform satisfactorily in employment. Or they do not accept the contention that in many public occupations, jobs could be more efficiently performed by less skilled labor, allowing for job redesign. Apart from a small number of surveys of programs, no study has been reported that has probed the economics of a division of labor sufficiently to offer conclusions relevant to the arguments for or against paraprofessional employment. For the case of the teaching profession, and especially for work in lower grades, this study provides some fundamental intelligence about the costs and benefits of teacher-paraprofessional work systems in education.

Focusing as it does on a compensatory education program for disadvantaged children, the study may also have some contribution to make to discussions about the value of federal-local programs to improve the educational achievement of "minority" children. In recent years, billions of dollars of federal funds have been granted to local school districts to permit them to enrich their educational efforts for ghetto students. Currently, however, decisionmakers at local and federal levels are discouraged about the achievements of these programs and the efficacy of continuing them when they appear to return small educational gains for funds expended. The conclusion that the educational benefits of the programs are not commensurate with expenditures has been stimulated by the conclusions of the Coleman report and similar studies.[1] This celebrated study of a national sample of schools examined relationships between educational achievement levels and characteristics of students, their families, teachers, and school programs, and concluded that there were only very weak relationships between student achievement and relative school expenditures. This denial that "money makes a difference" has sparked sharp debates about the merits of the study and the accuracy of its conclusions. But apart from the merits, the practical result has been gradual withdrawal of federal support for compensatory education programs.

A singular feature of the federal programs, the program evaluations, and conclusions drawn from them, is that neither the programs, the evaluations, nor conclusions ever examined in detail the nature of organized school processes by which inputs of federal money were supposed to be transformed into improved educational treatments to boost educational achievement in children. It is not true that federal funds were granted without some stipulations as to how they should be spent. But usually, funds were expended on the general assumption that money would make a difference although detailed plans for changing existing educational practices—those that were historically associated with low achievement for minorities—seldom were drawn up with the exception of a limited number of experimental programs.

The conclusion that compensatory education has failed, therefore, is based on experience with programs that utilized federal funding but that may not have changed educational practices sufficiently to test these questions. That Professor Coleman himself recognized this possibility is made clear in a remark that has been too little noted by critics of his report.[2]

[1] James S. Coleman et al., *Equality of Educational Opportunity* (Washington, D.C.: U.S. Government Printing Office, 1966).

[2] James S. Coleman, "Equality of Educational Opportunity, Reply to Bowles and Levin," *Journal of Human Resources* 3, no. 2 (Spring 1968): 246.

The results of the survey suggest that a far less simple relation than ordinarily supposed exists between the economic resources that go into education and the achievement that results.

They suggest that the ineffectiveness of schools in providing educational opportunity independent of that provided by the home lies in the very organization of the system of public education rather than the particular level of resources of the schools.

They suggest that, given the present organization of education in the United States, the marginal utility of expenditures for education as measured by increments of achievement is far less than it might be under other modes of organization. What these modes of organization might be, I can hardly say, but it might be possible to learn.

No one study that evaluates traditional and newer "modes of organization," in this case organizational modes for instruction, can answer the fundamental question raised in Professor Coleman's remarks. But until the processes by which schools deliver instruction to children are studied in detail, it will not be known if new and additional money inputs are actually used in the schools in ways that affect the amount and quality of instruction that children receive.

To anticipate study findings to some extent, the results of the teacher work studies in this investigation suggest that individual disadvantaged children receive so little instructional attention in a school day that it would be remarkable if they could make relative gains in achievement that could provide them with greater educational equality. These findings imply that funds expended for compensatory education do not trickle down to the classroom level in ways that affect the amount and intensity of instruction children receive under traditional instructional methods. Readers will be able to form their own view of this matter by reviewing the extensive data of the teacher and paraprofessional work studies in the chapters that follow.

We would hope that the information and methods developed in this study, in addition, may stimulate new efforts in research for productivity measurement. The principal reason that much needed productivity measures for white collar occupations have not been forthcoming is that the outputs produced in work are difficult to measure as end products. Typically the work performed is more in the nature of a transaction between workers and persons served. The transactions do not involve exchanges that are easily measurable in unit terms as productivity indexes require. But if conventional labor productivity indexes are difficult to design for many service occupations, what are the alternatives?

It would appear that where measurement of service work outputs is not practical, the recourse must be to design special measures of intermediate labor effectiveness that will have utility even while they do not link labor inputs to final output. This is the recourse taken in this study. We have designed a system for estimating the daily amounts of instructional and noninstructional work teachers perform, and the system is sufficiently standardized to be useful in other school settings. Because of the character of the method, the system cannot be used to obtain global measures of end product productivity for large worker populations. But the system may have considerable utility for work measurement for other researchers, program planners, and school staff.

Finally, the general purpose of this study is to contribute intelligence about manpower utilization in the schools. However, the value of the study may extend beyond any utility the results may have for researchers, educators, or persons concerned with policy and programs. In recent years, educators have become aware that analytical methods such as systems and cost benefit analysis may have considerable value for decisionmaking. Even so, there are not yet many investigations available to indicate what the value of these methods may be when they are focused at the level of institutions where people work. Despite any specific deficiencies, perhaps the research can provide a demonstration effect to stimulate further interest in the application of these analytical methods in public industries.

The Cost Effectiveness Perspective

This volume will be read by many persons who are not specialists and will not be familiar with methods of cost benefit analysis. For this reason, we have tried to reduce unnecessary technical formulations to a minimum throughout this book. At different places, where discussions of technical matters are necessary, we have preceded these discussions with brief nontechnical background statements for the benefit of nonspecialists. The following brief statement of perspectives in cost benefit analysis will be a useful preliminary to the study for these readers.

Cost benefit analysis is an approach to evaluating resource allocation that derives from more general perspectives about economic processes in society. This perspective assumes that in public or private affairs the wants of society exceed the resources available to satisfy those wants. Given these circumstances, it follows that managers and other decisionmakers will necessarily be making choices with efficiency implications when they allocate funds for new programs or for changing existing programs and practices.

In the cost benefit perspective, the terms "efficiency" and "economy" have special meaning. "Efficiency" does not necessarily imply that all resources should be spent for a one "best way" to accomplish program goals, nor does the term "economy" imply stringency. Proceeding from the assumption that wants exceed resources to achieve wants, a related assumption is that it is rational to design and operate programs that have the highest utility in terms of maximizing program objectives for resources expended. In this context, efficiency and economy are two ways of looking at the same characteristics of public or private programs. That is, for any specified objective or budget for a given program, the management choices that maximize attainment of a program objective for a given budget level (are "efficient") are those that minimize the cost of achieving those objectives (they are "economical"). There is interdependency between the two terms, because a program that is efficient and maximizes objectives cannot also be uneconomical and fail to minimize the costs of gaining the objectives.

The pursuit of efficiency goals dictates that managers should pursue the objective of obtaining the greatest satisfaction of wants given limited resources. Decisionmakers usually are confronted with many choices for resource expenditure options. Therefore, they should be constrained to consider the costs of program inputs and the value of program outputs in order to evaluate the net benefits that can be produced with alternative expenditure choices for programs. These perspectives indicate that resources for programs are most efficiently spent when the ratio of costs to benefits of all program expenditures is equal. The efficiency goal of attaining maximum benefits for given inputs for all investments requires that where this is not so, resources should be shifted from programs with lower cost benefit ratios to programs with higher ratios. Optimal expenditure practices for all programs would be obtained, therefore, when the added benefits for an additional dollar spent for all programs are equal.

Cost benefit analysis is an approach to evaluation of programs and decisions in the context of the foregoing statements. The term "cost benefit analysis" is a generic term, and it has no specific methodological referent. Instead, the term may refer to any number of approaches for identifying program cost and benefit ratios, or other estimates of program costs and payoffs. The analysis may be an activity that sums and compares the direct costs of program alternatives without using more abstract methods of measurement. More often, however, the approach will employ systems analysis and related quantitative techniques to assess benefits and costs by analytical testing and model building for program assumptions and results.

Regardless of special methods used, it is common in all cost benefit analysis to identify the benefits and costs of alternative program choices sufficiently so managers can make choices to gain the largest benefits for resources to be expended. Analyses will usually consist of several steps:

1. identification of program costs and program benefits;

2. expression of these benefits and costs in money terms;

3. estimation of net program benefits gained in relation to costs expended; and

4. comparison of present and future benefits that programs obtain over future time periods. In addition, investigations usually apply evaluation criteria to define net cost benefit ratios, pay back periods for resources invested in programs, marginal benefit ratios, and similar judgment criteria.

A conventional goal for cost benefit analysis is to express costs and benefits in money terms in order to determine the level of net benefits that programs return. This operation assumes that benefits of programs can be measured in money equivalents, but many programs produce benefits that cannot be measured in money terms. It may be possible to measure benefits commensurable with other unit scales of measurement, but the scales may not lend themselves to translation into dollar units.

In education it is often possible to estimate dollar costs of programs for children. Nevertheless, gains in learning achievement may be impossible to translate into commensurable monetary values. For some special populations of students this translation problem can be overcome, as when evaluations have examined the labor market and earnings experience of program graduates, and used indexes of employment and earnings as benefit measures. However, this study is concerned with educational experiences of elementary school children, and postschool employment is not a consideration for this young cohort.

An alternative to cost benefit analysis that is used when benefits cannot be expressed in money terms is cost effectiveness analysis. These analyses, unlike cost benefit analyses, attempt to evaluate programs by retaining benefit measurement indicators in their original form. Cost effectiveness methods identify costs, and relate costs to benefits, when benefits are expressed as direct program products without translation into money units of value. In education, such program benefits as student gains in achievement test scores may be related to costs of alternative possible educational programs.

Cost effectiveness analysis is not inferior to cost benefit analysis because benefits are not expressed in direct money unit terms. The choice for cost effectiveness analysis is simply dictated by the impossibility of translating some kinds of benefit values into financial terms. Cost effectiveness analysis can be an extremely useful method for providing decisionmakers with intelligence about the efficiency and benefit consequences of alternative program arrangements. The cost effectiveness analysis that, with the work productivity study, makes up this complete study is the first such analysis to examine details of educational labor at the school work place.

Organization of the Study

In research design, this study is divided into related substudies that examine teacher and paraprofessional work, their employment costs, and the educational consequences of their employment. Chapter 2 that follows discusses the general methodology of the study, including design and testing of the work study, and identifies particulars of the Portland, Oregon, school district where the study was performed.

The work study answers the question: What work do teachers and paraprofessionals perform, and what new patterns of labor inputs are produced, when they are teamed in the classroom division of labor? The study stands by itself as a first analysis of work in traditional and newer educational staffing systems. However, the essential purpose of the work study was to provide observations for the cost effectiveness analysis in the study.

When the research was in the planning stage, we hoped to be able to locate existing sources of empirical data that might identify dimensions of work that teachers and paraprofessionals perform in schools. If information of this kind was available, our intention was to use it for the models of the new division of work we required for the cost effectiveness analysis. However, this reveals our ignorance, at that time, of the status of work and productivity measurement in education. Unlikely as it will seem to persons who are familiar with the history of work and productivity measurement in private industry, in education no research has been done to develop work and productivity measurement schemes.

Consequently, a major part of the report is concerned with the methods and measurement results of our efforts to measure productive instructional work of teachers and paraprofessionals. Chapter 3 reports results of the work study that focused on teachers who worked alone in traditional, single-teacher, classroom arrangements. This teacher group was studied first in order to identify traditional work patterns, so that they could be compared later with work performed by teamed teachers and paraprofessionals.

Chapter 4 discusses the work study of teachers who were teamed with paraprofessionals in the Portland schools. In this study, as in the studies of paraprofessional and conventional teacher work, effort was made to distinguish between productive instructional work performed by staff and work expended in nonprofessional routine duties. The studies also identify the amount of daily time that the staff allocated to classwide instruction or instruction of the individual child as well as to different subject matter areas.

Chapter 5 reports results of the work study of paraprofessionals, compares their work output with that of teachers, and summarizes work comparisons for the teacher groups and paraprofessionals. This chapter concludes the part of the study that is concerned with empirical measurement of work results. However, empirical results from the work studies are incorporated into analytical cost effectiveness models in subsequent chapters.

Chapter 6 is concerned with cost analysis. Costs of the traditional and the new instructional systems are compared by deriving estimates of hourly instructional costs for both systems. The additional annual labor costs the school district experienced when paraprofessionals were introduced are identified. The information in this chapter, therefore, analyzes costs of employment on a unit labor cost basis and also examines more comprehensive annual costs of incorporating the teacher-paraprofessional work system into a school district.

A central goal of the study was to obtain work observations and employment cost data good enough in quality to permit quantitative modeling of the new division of labor. Chapter 7 uses data from the work and cost studies in a linear programming model that explores potential economies that may be obtainable in the new work system. The model utilizes linear programming methods to identify more optimal teacher and paraprofessional work assignment patterns; patterns that maximize joint teaching outputs of staff while labor costs are minimized. This chapter, therefore, presses the general analysis beyond the empirical and inductive focus of the work study.

Benefit measurement is achieved in the study by analysis of reading achievement scores of school children who attended the compensatory education program in which teacher-paraprofessional teams were employed. Chapter 8 discusses the statistical analyses of the third and fifth grade reading achievement scores that were developed in the research. The final pages of the report in Chapter 9 summarize conclusions from the work studies, the employment cost analyses, and the achievement test analyses, and present conclusions about cost effectiveness consequences of teacher-paraprofessional employment in the new school division of labor.

2 Research Methods

The objectives of this study were to measure the work produced by teachers and paraprofessionals and to identify the costs and benefits associated with their teamed employment in the division of labor in schools. At the study planning stage, it was anticipated that benefits of the new work system might include savings in employment costs, increased instructional productivity, and greater learning achievement gains for children instructed. This chapter discusses the methods used in each of the substudies of educational work, employment costs, and educational benefits that are included in the complete study.

Research Objectives and Setting

When the study was being planned, it was not certain that a study of manpower utilization practices with cost benefit design could be carried out in the schools. No major studies of the work teachers perform in schools had been completed to that time. It was not apparent that teachers would tolerate close study of their work. Nor was it certain that school districts would keep cost information adequate for a study. No previous research had been performed that tested research difficulties in these areas. Therefore, several questions about requirements for study design were of immediate concern.

A priority matter was that of identifying adequate analytical models for the analysis: models that would determine the kind of empirical data the investigation would require. Both economic theory and the history of industrial experience suggested that education was recapitulating experience in other industries where, for efficiency reasons, paraprofessionals and professionals have been teamed at work. Consequently, an appropriate approach for the study appeared to be one directed at determining if the new division of labor obtained efficiencies due to specialization patterns it introduced in instructional work.

In particular, this perspective dictated that the investigation should be designed to establish (1) if the work that paraprofessionals performed was of sufficient value to justify economic costs of their employment; (2) if teacher professionals performed more specialized and valuable work when aides were employed; and (3) if the new division of labor produced educational benefits that justified costs of the new work system. These central questions for analysis indicated that an appropriate methodology would concentrate on (a) identifying any new productive work contributed by teachers and paraprofessionals;

13

(b) identifying and evaluating costs of the new work division, presumably principally labor costs; and (c) measuring any learning achievement gains of students that were attributable to new labor inputs from the new work specialization.

A first question about research design that required an answer before research proceeded was the question: Could districts be identified that employed teachers and paraprofessionals in instructional programs with sufficient formal structure so that programs could be effectively evaluated? This question had key implications for research design. The teacher-paraprofessional work division is emerging in the schools. Many districts could be identified where administrators were pursuing the objective of work specialization. However, newly established work programs might not be sufficiently settled in their operations so the study could examine parameters stable enough for measurement. Another consideration was that the study could focus on programs in several districts for comparative purposes. The choice was finally made to perform the investigation in the metropolitan school district of Portland, Oregon, for several reasons.

In the late 1960s, an extensive survey was made to establish the character of school district programs for employment of teachers and paraprofessionals. A key finding was that, at that time, most smaller nonmetropolitan districts were still initiating or expanding employment of nonprofessionals. The data indicated that larger, metropolitan districts had more rationally structured programs for nonprofessional employment in their compensatory programs for inner city children. The survey and other investigations also indicated that districts differed remarkably in terms of the quality of accounting and other data they could provide for analyses. Again, the metropolitan districts had information systems that offered data superior in quality and amount.

The choice to perform the investigation in School District Number One in Portland, Oregon, was made because most of the considerations noted were satisfied in this city setting. When the study was initiated in the fall of 1968, the district had employed many paraprofessionals for several years. All indications were that the district program for employing paraprofessionals was representative of programs in other major cities. Moreover, the district could provide adequate cost data and offered an effective achievement testing program that contained longitudinal data from several annual testing cycles. Subsequently, the cost and test score data proved invaluable for the research effort.

The Portland district is the metropolitan district, and with an enrollment of 77,000 students, it is 26th in enrollment rank in the nation. From the mid 1960s, the district has operated a program for compensatory education for disadvantaged children in nine elementary schools in the low-income section of the city. It is in these nine schools that employment of district paraprofessionals has been concentrated. In Portland, as in many other large city districts, the goal of obtaining more intensive remedial instruction for disadvantaged children has stimulated employment of paraprofessional instructors. Because of this, the study could focus on analysis of the new division of labor in a setting where remedial objectives were being pursued and considerations of social relevance for research were well met.

The schools included in the study are all located in or near a ghetto area predominantly populated by low-income black families. The children who attend these schools experience those general life circumstances all too familiar for impoverished children. Many more of them suffer from inadequate nutrition, broken homes, and other forms of deprivation than do children in other areas of the city. They also experience educational handicaps common to low-income children in the nation's inner cities: during the 1960s, average achievement test scores for the children in this area were at least one grade level below the all-city average, depending on the grade in question.

The district compensatory education program had the objective of reducing educational achievement disadvantages of these children by providing more intensive remedial instruction and other supporting services. In support of the remedial objective, teacher-pupil ratios were reduced from a district average of approximately twenty-five students to twenty students to one professional teacher. Curriculum materials were also expanded, and administrative support was increased, as were counseling services. However, the most unusual departure from customary practices was introduction of teaching paraprofessionals into the teaching division of labor and their assignment to teachers. This innovation further reduced the effective teacher-pupil ratio in those hours when teachers and their aides were teamed together so that ratios of instructors to children were then more like one to ten.

Teaching paraprofessionals were first employed in significant numbers in the district in 1965. District managers at that time made the decision to expend most of their resources for paraprofessionals in two sections of the district. The district is administratively divided into several sections called "Areas," and the ghetto area, which will be termed Area I in this report, received the larger proportion of all paraprofessional assignments. In Area I, principals of schools received enough new positions so they could assign paraprofessionals at a ratio of one assistant to every two teachers at lower grade levels. Alternatively, they could assign paraprofessionals to three or four teachers and spread their assignments over grades one through six.

In three of the nine schools in Area I, principals limited assignment of paraprofessionals to grades one to four. In those grades, they were assigned to work for two teachers who taught at the same grade level. These three schools where paraprofessionals were assigned to grades one to four were attended almost entirely by black children. For many years, the schools had the lowest student achievement records in the district. The six other Area I schools were in neighborhoods that were changing from white to black populations during the 1960s. At the beginning of that decade, when these six schools had predominantly white enrollment, student achievement levels were not very different from levels found in other city schools. By the mid 60s, school achievement levels had begun to decline as black enrollment increased at all grade levels. In these six Area I schools, which will be referred to as "changing schools," principals allocated assignments of paraprofessionals more thinly across grade levels. In these schools, the usual practice was to assign paraprofessionals to three to five teachers and to grades one through eight.

The explanation for this difference in assignment practices is linked to enrollment characteristics in Area I schools. In the three schools with largely black enrollment, principals chose to concentrate staff resources in grades one to four on the assumption that remedial education was most effectively concentrated in the early learning years. The principals in the six changing schools, however, were influenced by other problems. Their principal need was for a more dense distribution of staff over all grade levels to maintain school order and instruction as enrollment change processes crossed all grades.

This pattern of differential staff assignment in the black enrollment and changing schools influenced study findings about achievement gains students made in the compensatory program. To anticipate the findings to some extent, the analysis established that students received more instruction and registered achievement gains in the three schools where paraprofessionals were assigned to two teachers. In the six Area I schools, where changes in composition of enrollment were under way and paraprofessionals were assigned to as many as five teachers, the achievement gains were less pronounced and were not maintained longitudinally. The achievement score analysis in Chapter 8 reports details of these differences.

Most, but not all, of the research effort was concentrated in Area I in the Portland district. A subsidiary goal of the research was to determine how paraprofessionals were utilized in diverse school settings. Also, it seemed worthwhile to determine if work patterns of teachers and paraprofessionals differed when the staff was not employed in compensatory educational programs. Teachers and paraprofessionals were also employed in Portland schools in the district's Area II, a section of the district where students were from white, middle, and lower middle-income student populations. Some of the work study observations in this report were obtained by study of teachers and paraprofessionals who were employed in schools in Area II.

The initial intention when these subjects were included was to establish if staff work patterns in nonghetto schools were similar to work patterns observed in the compensatory program in Area I schools. Moreover, it appeared at the time Area II staff were included that achievement test results for Area II children would be available for purposes of benefit analysis. This subsequently proved not to be true because the tests available were not suitable for research purposes. Nevertheless, the work observations for Area II staff were useful for study purposes because they allowed the analysis to determine that in conventional school operations, where compensatory programs are not operating, the new teacher and paraprofessional work division produced instruction much in excess of the conventional, single-teacher, division of labor.

Additional details about the rationale for selecting the schools and subjects that were included in the study are contained in Appendix B. That appendix also provides information about characteristics of subjects who were studied in the work analysis. It also reports some statistical analyses of personal characteristics and of work produced by teacher and paraprofessional populations, analyses that were performed to determine if the study populations differed significantly in terms of intergroup work results and demographic characteristics.

The research effort extended over the period from June 1968 until Winter 1971. During this period, the several substudies that make up the investigation were carried out. Of these, the one that required the most extensive field effort was the study of teacher and paraprofessional work tasks performed in the new division of labor. Other analyses included the linear programming study of instructional work, the achievement test analysis to estimate educational benefits produced by the educational program, and the data collection and analysis for the study of teacher and paraprofessional employment costs. The methods of each of these substudies are discussed below. Additional details can be found in Appendixes A and B.

Identification of Costs

In ideal form, cost effectiveness studies should measure all costs associated with program activities and identify all benefits that result from expenditures. By definition, if important benefits and costs are omitted from analysis, the efforts can produce information of limited value for decisionmakers. In practice, it is often not possible, for theoretical and practical reasons, to achieve comprehensive cost and benefit identification and measurement. Practical difficulties often impede data collection and measurement efforts. Concerning theory, specialists themselves often disagree about appropriate cost and benefit concepts and methods for analysis.

Given these realities, an appropriate response is to recognize that careful partial analyses can provide valuable information for decisionmaking. Moreover, assuming study findings are carefully proscribed where data must be omitted, analysts may acquit themselves well. It seldom is necessary to have "full" information for purposes of deciding that one program alternative is more efficient than another. In this study, we have been able to identify relevant costs of employing teacher-paraprofessional teams rather well. As we subsequently note, comprehensive benefit measurement was more difficult to achieve.

The cost analysis model used in this study compares the labor costs and work productivity of the teacher-paraprofessional work system with the costs and productivity of conventional, single-teacher, work arrangements. Cost effectiveness analysis is typically concerned with reviewing results that can be achieved by alternative program arrangements. The logical comparative focus for this study was one that compares costs and benefits of the new and the traditional work systems for classrooms. With regard to costs, there are at least three categories of costs that are relevant to this study.

The first category of costs that required identification were costs the district experienced for hiring paraprofessionals and bringing them into employment. These will be termed hiring costs. In addition, for many reasons it was useful to identify the costs of employing teachers and paraprofessionals that the district experienced on a basis of wages per hour worked. These hourly rates were readily calculable from district salary records for staff. These rate data were used in conjunction with work productivity observations from the work study to compute hourly instructional costs of the district. In addition to hiring cost and hourly rate data, information from district annual budgets was used to compute figures for annual district costs of instruction per attending child. From these annual average costs per child it was possible to determine the average annual costs per child of teacher and paraprofessional instruction.

In the course of the research, several investigations were pursued to identify any additional costs the district experienced as a consequence of employing paraprofessionals. With the cooperation of the district personnel office, personnel files were examined, recruiting channels were studied, and interviews were held across the district to determine what additional recruiting, induction, and training costs were experienced when paraprofessionals were employed. These probes established that only trivial costs were expended for recruiting and training paraprofessionals.

District personnel records indicated that for as long as paraprofessionals had been hired, there had been at least fifty job applicants for every job vacancy. Given these labor supply parameters, the district experienced only minor costs of recruiting and trivial costs of opening personnel records when aides were hired. Training costs were minimized because training was done on the job. Moreover, the costs of maintaining positions at schools were slight. No principal estimated that indirect costs of paraprofessional employment were more than $40 per year. In none of the schools were equipment stocks or facilities significantly modified as a consequence of paraprofessional employment.

These facts indicated the study could consider salary costs as the only significant costs of paraprofessional employment and omit other minor costs as trivial to the analysis. In larger perspective, what these cost explorations indicated was that the district had available a very large supply of local female labor that could be placed on the job at near zero cost and compensated at salaries approximately one half the level of professional teachers. This is to say that if administrators were satisfied that paraprofessionals' work was at all comparable to teachers' work in quality, then the economics of employing paraprofessionals certainly provided incentives to employ them.

The uses that were made of the cost information referred to are as follows. The hourly wage rate data were used with observations from the teacher and paraprofessional work study to establish the hourly, unit costs of producing hours of instruction for children. This analysis, reported in Chapter 6, then compared the relative costs of producing unit instructional hours when conventional or teacher-paraprofessional instructional systems were used. This first cost analysis provided information about the efficiency of the two work systems at the level of the production system. The linear programming analysis in Chapter 7 also used the wage cost and work study observations, but did so to explore a hypothetical model of an instructional work system. In that model, hourly labor cost and work study variables are manipulated to explore labor cost and work output parameters for a model school with hypothetical enrollment, budget, staffing, and other characteristics. The model solution determines an optimal assignment mix for teacher and paraprofessional labor, given stated levels of hourly labor costs, hourly work inputs, and other constraints stated in the model.

Measurement of Benefits

Costs of elements of the new division of work were not difficult to identify, but more substantial analytical problems were encountered in designing adequate measures of benefits of the new work system. Authorities are in unanimous agreement concerning the difficulty of obtaining comprehensive and precise measures of benefits of educational programs. Schools are among the foremost of our institutions that educate and socialize children. However, there is no ready consensus about objectives and benefits that education should achieve. Even if consensus could be obtained on the principle that cognitive development is the central objective of schooling, opinions would differ concerning the nature of cognitive development schools should foster. In fact, schools confer diverse benefits to individuals and society as a consequence of their programs. Social skills, formation of attitudes, and an extremely varied list of school program "outputs," in addition to cognitive skills, can be attributed to school activities.

Because they are the only standardized measures of school attainments, achievement tests have been the conventional measures of program benefits of schooling. The principal benefit indicators this study uses are reading achievement test results that were available for district children. Throughout the study, we considered many variables that might be considered as potential benefit indicator variables. At substantial effort, it might have been possible to originate such indicators as morale indexes for staff or children. And some existing data, such as attendance and turnover statistics, might have been utilized. However, only very complicated multivariate analyses might have identified any association between paraprofessional employment and attendance, turnover, or other benefit indicators. Limitations of research resources and estimates of the value of results for the study plan indicated that such indirect benefit measurements were not worth pursuing.

The reading achievement test scores that were used for benefit measurement purposes were obtained from the district's longitudinal achievement test program. For most years in the 1960s, the district had tested all children in the third and fifth grades in late Spring of each year with McMenemy tests of reading achievement. The availability of reading scores was especially propitious because in compensatory education programs, and in the program of this district, remedial reading instruction had high priority among program activities.

Some disadvantages associated with these sources of test score data—disadvantages we went to elaborate lengths to overcome—were as follows. A first drawback was that children were tested only once during third or fifth grade years. Therefore, no test results were available that could be used to measure "before and after" learning experience achieved between the beginning and end of any given year. Consequently, the more effective experimental designs for measuring pre- and posttreatment results for subjects was not available to us.

A second problem was that all children in the compensatory program received some instruction that was provided by the new teacher-paraprofessional teaming system. Therefore, in Area I, there were no students available who could be assigned to a control group for comparison and measurement. Faced with these practical difficulties, our choice was either to devise some extraordinary means of making controlled evaluations or quit the effort to measure educational results of the compensatory instructional program. The following very "strong" expedient was devised; one that utilized all district third grade scores for all years 1965 to 1970, plus fifth grade scores for 1970.

All test scores for all district third grade children for those six years were recorded on computor tape. Then reading achievement scores for Area I children in the compensatory education program were separated from scores of all other district third graders. The method used then analyzed the score levels of Area I children in the years before and after the program was established. In these analyses, longitudinal trends of reading scores of Area I children were also compared to the trends of scores of all other district children for comparison-control purposes. It was a matter of record that achievement score averages in the district—independent of Area I—had been declining slightly in the 1960s. It was also a matter of record that average scores in Area I had been in a trend of decline in the early 60s.

Our assumption was that if the Area I trend of score averages improved for the years after the program was initiated, and did so "against" the general district trend of decline, then this Area I trend would be evidence of program effectiveness. No other educational or demographic change was operating in Area I that could explain improvement in achievement trends, if it indeed was identified. In fact, as later discussion will detail, the trend of neighborhood residential changes in Area I created qualitative shifts in new student enrollments that were decidedly unfavorable for any program efforts to demonstrate average student achievement gains.

While it would have been preferable to design test score analyses that compared scores for instructed and noninstructed student groups from the same population of children, the method used in this study conferred a number of special advantages. First, the method of establishing comparison-controls by reviewing annual scores within the Area I populations, and with complete district populations, provides comprehensive review of achievement shifts in the populations. And with such extensive review, it was possible to achieve longitudinal measurements that program evaluations seldom achieve. For example, the 1970 fifth grade test scores used in the analysis were scores from the same student population that had been tested for reading achievement in 1968 in the third grade. The study was consequently able to identify fifth grade children who had been tested earlier in the third grade and determine if those children had improved or regressed in comparison to earlier third grade scores. Chapter 8, which reports the benefit analysis, identifies other innovations associated with the method.

The principal problem in measurement that the study could not overcome was the problem of specifically associating education benefits with direct teaching inputs of the new teacher-paraprofessional instructional system. The most desirable result for the study was to determine coefficients between units of new instruction produced, costs of that instruction, and unit measures of achievement gains children experienced as a result of instruction. However, for a number of reasons it was not possible to measure instruction units, cost units, and achievement units in a manner appropriate to multivariate analyses.

Measures of instructional costs and student achievement were available or could be devised. However, even the extensive work study data we collected could not produce measures of instruction, or proxy measures, that were appropriate for an analysis. An analysis to determine relationships between instruction and achievement would require that the empirical observations used to measure instruction be distributed over an extremely complex sampling frame to insure that observations were taken throughout the year for which children were to be tested. Thus, observations needed to be gathered in a time frame, and from sufficient class situations, to be representative of instruction during the grade-year children were taught. Even in the relatively comprehensive work study we performed for this research it was not practical to so distribute the observations made.

Because of these problems our recourse for studying the relationship between the amount of new instruction provided by teachers and paraprofessionals and student achievement was of the following kind. The work study was designed to determine what amounts of instruction newly teamed staff contributed to classroom instruction. We are sure the data gathered adequately measure this instruction. But the observation data could not be obtained within a distributed, annual time frame that would make the data suitable for multivariate analysis. However, as subsequent pages indicate, the study established that the new instructional system produced much more instruction, especially remedial reading instruction, than did single teacher arrangements that were in effect before the compensatory program was initiated.

Furthermore, results of the achievement test analysis indicate that children made achievement gains only after the new instructional system was introduced into the Area I program. These results do not establish a specific association between the increased instruction measured and the achievement gains. They also do not preclude the possibility that other factors could have influenced achievement levels. However, at the interface between instructors and disadvantaged children where reading was taught, the only important variable that was changed by the program was the amount and intensity of instruction that was brought about through use of the teacher-paraprofessional instructional system.

Accordingly, while specific coefficients could not be obtained to measure relationships between instruction and achievement, the weight of evidence from the work study, the test analysis, and analysis of program features indicates that the new division of labor was the principal factor which produced improvement in student achievement.

Design of the Work Study

Early in the planning period for this study, it became apparent that an extensive original study would have to be performed to identify the work that teachers and paraprofessionals perform in schools. The cost effectiveness study required that work parameters of the new work division be identified for cost analysis purposes. We had hoped to locate existing measurement studies that might give some reliable clues about the possible statistical distributions of elements of teacher work. If this kind of information had been available, it could have been used to form initial hypotheses about the distributions of work tasks that were performed by the populations. However, extensive searches and communications with educators indicated that to date there had been no satisfactory study identifying the work that teachers perform in schools.

A study of teacher and paraprofessional work was needed to provide data that could answer the following questions: First, what productive work do paraprofessionals perform in schools? Second, what productive work do teachers perform when paraprofessionals are assigned to them, and what tasks in comparison to those that teachers do alone in conventional arrangements? Third, does efficient specialization occur when paraprofessionals are assigned to work with teachers? That is, are teachers freed to perform more professional work, and do paraprofessionals assume the nonprofessional tasks of teachers? Fourth, do children receive different instructional treatments when the division of labor is specialized? Do they receive more instruction, and more intensive, individual instruction?

Three central problems required resolution in the design of work study methods that might be devised to answer these questions. The first problem was to define teacher and paraprofessional daily work tasks with operational, categorical definitions. The second was to design instruments that could be used in classrooms to observe and measure the defined work categories adequately for study purposes. Finally, it was necessary to insure that any work study methods designed could be used in schools to obtain representative observations from subjects. Observations were required of the work of three populations: teachers working with paraprofessionals, teachers working in conventional class arrangements, and paraprofessionals. The grade levels of concern were grades one to four because most paraprofessionals were assigned to these grades in Portland.

The initial design problem was to originate definitions of work categories to identify the work teachers and paraprofessionals perform. These work definitions would be used by classroom observers who would code subject work activities. There were two methods of approach available for developing and proving these work category definitions. One alternative was to perform a series of field studies where alternative definitions of work were tested in observation studies. The codings of work that were produced could then be analyzed by factor analysis or similar methods to define dimensions of teacher work. However, this direction of approach promised to be complex, time consuming, and burdened with hazards. The foremost of these was the possibility that the analysis might identify work category definitions that could not be operationalized for subsequent use by observers.

A second, alternative empirical method was open to us. This was that categorical definitions of work tasks could be devised a priori after drawing on results of discussions with teachers and experts. These definitions, designed to include all instructional and noninstructional work of the school staff, could then be tested in field trials where two or more observers were assigned to single subjects. If the interobserver reliability for coding was very high, this would be a satisfactory demonstration of the reliability and face validity of the method and work definitions. This was the alternative for developing and proving work study methods that was elected.

The development of the definitions to be used by work observers was the most important aspect of the work study design. The nature of phenomena to be observed, the anticipated method to be used for making observations, and the need for reliability, all affected the choice of definitions. But, in addition to these considerations, definitions were required that would have such high face validity and universality that they would be useful to other investigators. Having discovered ourselves that no adequate methods existed to measure productive and nonproductive work of teachers, we wanted to design a plan that could satisfy the needs of other users in the future.

A first required characteristic of the definitions, therefore, was that they be such straightforward references to such obvious and universal features of teacher work that observers, in busy school environments, could readily perceive the defined tasks. The anticipated observational plan was to assign observers to school staff during the day and have them code work tasks with teachers or paraprofessionals as the focus of observation. The observers would follow work progress and record the minutes daily that staff expended in instructional and noninstructional work. Working under these circumstances, observers would require definitions that were uncomplicated and required a minimum of ad hoc classification decisions.

Concerning the work tasks that would be identified by the definitions, an important consideration was that tasks be defined as having attributes of professional or nonprofessional work. It proved not to be difficult to develop clear distinctions between professional and nonprofessional work. Among educators we talked to, there was general agreement that instructional tasks of teachers were the most valued, professional, and productive work that existed in the profession. No educator failed to also note that much of the working time of teachers was occupied with unproductive, nonprofessional work of routine character. There was also consensus that much of this routine work of a noninstructional character was work that paraprofessionals could very well perform. These discussions led us to establish definitions for "Instruction" and "Routine" work categories.

In the study and analysis we defined the work time that staff expended in this Instruction category as the productive work time that is produced in the division of labor for teaching. This equating of Instruction, as we measured it, with the productive work of the division did not appear to be arbitrary, although in this usage the term has a different connotation than is usual in economic analysis. No measurement of instruction we might have devised could have accomplished the difficult goal of linking "end products" of instruction with labor inputs as conventional productivity measurement does. It is hardly clear what the "end products" of education are. However, our definition of time spent in instruction as an "intermediate" productivity measurement has utility for efficiency analysis purposes. The measurement of instructional time, moreover, quantifies an important dimension of the division of labor that educators value very highly.

The definitions for instruction and routine work were defined broadly to include a large number of teaching and routine tasks and were considered comprehensive of work in those categories. In fact, the purposes of this study could have been accomplished if the work study instruments had been designed to measure only time expended on instruction and routine work, with all other work defined in one other general category. This triple classification scheme would have told us most of what we wanted to know about teacher and paraprofessional work. However, for several reasons it was desirable to have a more elaborate work measurement breakdown.

One of these reasons was that we wanted to establish what amount of time teachers and paraprofessionals spent during school hours planning their work and interacting with each other. If the teachers' total planning time and time interacting with other staff was increased by having paraprofessionals assigned to them, then it would be important to consider this in evaluating the new division of work. For this reason a work activity category "Aide" was included in the category definitions. Observers were to use this category to identify the daily time during which teachers and paraprofessionals interacted in consultations and other activities.

The remaining work categories defined were designated "Nonlearning," "Evaluation," and "Planning." These were included after discussions with teachers and pretrials established they were needed to define comprehensively the work activities of staff. All sources indicated that planning and evaluation functions were important elements of teachers' work. The planning category was defined to include all classroom planning and preparation for work that personnel performed. The evaluation category was meant to cover all situations where teachers and paraprofessionals corrected student work or otherwise evaluated student behavior.

Our inquiries also pointed to a great deal of classroom activity of instructional staff that is spent in purposes that have no direct educational objective; staff and students socialize, perform ceremonies, and other kinds of activites that are not related to formal or informal curricula. To embrace these activities, including discipline, the category Nonlearning was established. This definition did not imply, of course, that no general human learning took place during Nonlearning activites. The point was that no formal or informal educational objectives were associated with behavior coded for this category.

When category definitions and coding instruments were readied, the coding processes were first pretested in elementary schools in our university school district. The trials established that it was possible to be in a classroom all day with teachers, perform work coding, and not be so conspicuous as to upset school routines. The test results were reviewed extensively and minor changes were made to improve coding reliability. The course then followed was to begin study in the Portland schools while continuous evaluations of the work study results were performed. In practice, this meant that early in the field work we periodically assigned two observers to code the work subject during the school day so information for intercoder reliability studies would be maintained. Details of these reliability studies are reported in Appendix A. Here we note only that for those categories in which staff expended most of their work time, observers averaged between 80 and 90 percent coding agreement for the minutes of work they assigned to the categories.

Work Study Coding Categories

The work study categories that were used in the research included the following:

Instruction activities (Code symbol IN): time spent by teacher or paraprofessionals in activities with a curriculum or general educational purpose. Learning-based interactions between subject and children are the events that provide the basis for coding.

Observers coded IN and the time expended in IN activities when paraprofessionals and teachers were observed in the defined activites. The following activities were the principal activities observers coded:

Lecture	Group learning discussions	Drill
Recitation	Student learning conferences	Demonstrations
Desk-to-desk help	Lesson plan instructions	Reading
Individual help	Performance instructions	

Routine activities (ROUT): time expended in activities that require little or no professional training. Clerical, materials handling, and monitoring tasks are heavily represented. Representative activities were:

Material handling	Housekeeping
Equipment operation	Student control
Class passing monitoring	Proctor tests
Clerical recording	Duplicate materials
Collect funds	

Nonlearning activities (NONL): time spent in class activities that have no direct educational-curriculum content. Representative activities were:

Opening ceremonies	Interruptions
Announcements	Assignments
Discipline	

The following activities were included when they were not instructional and staff were not dealing with educational content:

Group Planning	Student activities	General discussions

Planning activities (PLAN): teacher or paraprofessionals engaged in class and lesson planning. This category includes only planning by teacher or aide alone or with other school staff:

Lesson planning	Planning discussions
Class schedules	Plan class materials

Evaluation activities (EVAL): teacher or paraprofessionals activity in correcting papers, tests, and in evaluation of students and methods alone or with other staff.

Administrative activities (ADMIN): activities performed related to school administrative operations, district testing programs, or provision of technical-professional assistance to other professionals.

In addition to the above categories, which were used to measure work tasks, the following categories were used to code for teacher paraprofessional interactions and for free time or inactive time:

Inactive time: (INACT): Inactive time was recorded for teacher or paraprofessional situations in class when either is idle or relaxing.

Paraprofessional-teacher interactions (AIDE): Time expended for all reasons by teacher or paraprofessional in interaction with each other for planning work, consulting, or other reasons.

Out-of-class time (OUT): Teacher or paraprofessionals out of class for free time, personal time, and in transition to class.

In addition to these major activity classes, observers recorded the following subject matter and teacher-pupil interaction codes whenever teachers or paraprofessionals were engaged in IN (Instructional) activities only. The result obtained is a detailed coding that indicates if IN activities were devoted to language arts, math, or other subjects, and if the basis of instruction was individual student-small group, or entire class focused. These codes for designating curriculum areas and teacher class interaction bases for IN were:

Curriculum Code for IN:
R for language arts
M for math-numerical
A for arts
O for other

Curriculum Code for Staff-Class Interaction:
1 for staff interaction with individual students or small groups (one to six students)
2 for staff interaction with entire class

Selection of Subjects

Our pretests of our instruments established that they could obtain reliable observations of the subjects' work, but a final problem to resolve was that of insuring that the observations would be distributed over representative subjects and at representative times when they worked. This problem was very difficult to resolve because of the extremely complex situational factors associated with the nature of and time schedules of school work. For example, variance in tasks performed might occur by time of day, day of week, and other time dimensions. Our original plan was to sample blocks of teacher and paraprofessional work time during school days. This might have insured that representative work tasks were observed according to daily dimensions. Sampling of schools and subjects was also an objective.

However, strict sampling plans were abandoned for two reasons. First, no information existed that could be used to identify hypothetical sampling parameters for sampling schemes. Moreover, it became obvious that sampling plans for schools, work hours, and subjects would create complicated school visiting and observation schedules. It did not seem possible that observers could move in and out of schools and classes according to a sampling plan and not disrupt schools.

Because of these problems, we finally decided to "overwhelm" the problem by making observations of long enough duration with enough subjects so that we might have confidence that the observations were measuring average work tendencies. To insure that work observations would be comprehensive across the daily work tasks of staff, the procedure adopted was to assign observers to teachers or paraprofessionals for a full work day each. And to insure that we did not introduce bias into the selection of staff, we included in the study all the teachers and paraprofessionals in grades one to four in eight Portland elementary schools.

These selections did not guarantee that there would be no biases in observation data, but for several reasons we believe the data are representative of work in the schools of the district. Our explorations established that school schedules, curricula, and teacher general duties were sufficiently uniform across the district so that program features in particular schools were not likely to cause significant variance in work patterns. Other probes reported in Appendix B supported the conclusion that staff in the different schools were quite homogeneous in terms of characteristics one might hypothesize would influence work performance. But perhaps the best evidence is that our strategy of massing observations toward central tendencies that might exist appears to have worked.

In the second year of the field work, observers returned to the schools and performed a more modest work study. In this study they observed single staff members for only one hour during the day. They took care to distribute the hours of observation for all staff members evenly over the whole school day. The results of this briefer study were that the average number of minutes that staff spent in work categories such as Instruction and Routine were very close to averages obtained in the more extensive work study of the previous year. It proved possible, in other words, to visit a group of subjects one year later, sample their work only one hour each per day, and replicate work averages obtained a year earlier in observations of a total day. These results, which are reported in Appendix B, suggest the work study method and subject selection procedures produced results substantially representative according to subject and work schedule criteria.

The schools where the study was performed were three Portland Area I schools with nearly 100 percent black enrollment, and five Area II schools with enrollments from primarily white, middle-class neighborhoods. The black enrollment schools were included so the work of teacher paraprofessional teams with severely disadvantaged children could be studied. The inclusion of the Area II schools allowed the research to include teachers and paraprofessionals that worked under more conventional school conditions with white majority children.

The work study, therefore, was performed in eight Portland schools in 1968-69, and a more modest study was carried out in 1969-70 to validate the method. All the teachers and paraprofessionals that worked in grades one to four were observed at work for one full day. A total of twenty-seven teachers who worked with paraprofessionals were observed in Area I and II schools. Twenty-eight paraprofessionals were studied. Twenty teachers from Area II schools who worked in conventional class arrangements without paraprofessionals were also included. Studies that were made of relationships between subject work patterns and influences of personal or institutional variables on these patterns are reported in Appendix B.

3

Teacher Work in Conventional Classroom Roles

In private industry, the details of occupational work processes have been studied for decades. The reasons for this attention to work measurement are not difficult to detail. A large part of the increases in productivity that are associated with industrial development are the result of continual study within industries of means to employ labor more efficiently. In the private sector, an ordinary expectation for managerial performance is the norm that managers will routinely monitor work and work methods for efficiency purposes.

The situation has not been the same in public education. The basic facts that could detail the work that teachers perform in classes are not known. Only very general expectations exist that define satisfactory work outcomes. This situation is all the more remarkable because educational managers have often expressed dissatisfaction with traditional school work arrangements and their apparent consequences. Teachers also have frequently complained that their work is burdened with tasks that leave them little time to teach. The work study reported in this and the following chapters identifies details of work and confirms some causes of these expressions of dissatisfaction.

The work of elementary school teachers who worked in conventional classroom work arrangements was studied first in our research to provide norms of comparison for subsequent analysis of the work of teachers who worked with paraprofessionals. As we have indicated, the research plan was to study and compare the work patterns of teacher groups to determine if teachers who worked with paraprofessionals performed comparably more specialized, professional work, or otherwise achieved more valuable work outcomes. The twenty teachers whose work is identified in this chapter worked in grades one to four in elementary classrooms and in schools that were, in general, typical of those in public education settings in America. Teachers were responsible for the annual, in-grade education of one class of approximately twenty-five children. Within a framework of general school district policies and curriculum goals, they worked rather autonomously in the classroom and could determine their own teaching methods and work pace within daily schedules. Students in their classes were largely from white, middle- or lower middle-income families, and their tested achievement levels approximated the average for the school district.

The work observation results for these twenty teachers were obtained by observers who attended school for a full work day with each teacher. Observers entered classes at the beginning of the school day and coded teacher activities until children left school for the day. The total daily time for observations, therefore, was five and one-half hours which included one-half hour of teacher free time. Work that teachers performed in periods of the day before and after classes met was not observed. However, teachers were asked to estimate the amounts of nonclass time that were spent in class preparations and other school-related work. These estimates were not included in the tables of observed work time reported in this or later chapters.

When observations were made, observers coded the time that teachers spent in the several activity categories devised for the study. These categories, as Chapter 2 has indicated, identified time expended in instruction and routine work, and also nonlearning, planning, evaluation, administrative, inactive, aide, and out-of-class activities. Moreover, coders also recorded time teachers expended in the curriculum areas of language arts, math (or numerical instruction), and art. It is worth stressing that teachers and not students were the focus for observation. Observers did not direct attention to children except as was necessary to determine what was the purpose of teacher activity.

However, the observation methods used required that observers note if interaction between teachers and students during instruction activities took place on a classwide or individual-small group basis. The result is that all observations for instruction are identifiable, first, according to their curriculum coding for language arts, math, or art. Second, the teacher-class interaction basis for these instruction components is also defined because of the interaction coding. The results from the complete observation procedure provide a very detailed breakdown of teacher activity during the school day when children attended classes.

Before study results are reported, the point should be made that in none of the subsequent discussion where teacher work results are cited as being relatively "lower" or "higher" in productive work is there an implication that more work might have been produced if teacher effort had been greater. The kind of observation results we have do not permit inferences that individuals worked with more or less merit because they produced more or less measured work on the day they were observed. The teaching day of particular teachers may be interrupted by convocations, conferences, and other matters that defer instruction. Presumably some teachers experienced losses of instructional opportunity on days they were studied for just these reasons. However, these disturbances would not have an undesirable result on average work times the study obtained for the entire group of teachers. In fact, for the group averages, what we wished to know was what amounts of instructional and noninstructional time teachers spent in representative work days when these interruptions would occur among the group with normal frequency.

Teacher Instruction per Day

The first work study results to be examined are results for the amount of time per day that teachers expended in instruction. Table 3-1 presents the work study

Table 3-1
Daily Minutes Expended in Instructional Time (IN) and Curriculum Subcategories of IN, Including Class Interaction Basis, Twenty Teachers Working Conventionally

Teacher Number	Teacher Daily Minutes of Individual and Small Group Language Arts Instruction	Teacher Daily Minutes of Individual and Small Group Math Instruction	Teacher Daily Minutes of Individual and Small Group Art Instruction	Teacher Daily Minutes of Classwide Language Arts Instruction	Teacher Daily Minutes of Classwide Math Instruction	Teacher Daily Minutes of Classwide Art Instruction	Other	Teacher Total Daily Instructional Time
1	20.58	8.00		49.95	23.92			102.45
2	22.11	5.51		47.14	18.03		39.44	132.23
3	60.00	7.67		42.83	5.58		25.50	141.58
4	43.29			17.70		4.23		65.22
5	73.86	21.25		14.66	2.00		12.75	124.52
6	7.68			41.20				48.88
7	52.17	.75						52.92
8	11.01	5.83		6.83	31.25	4.17	26.83	85.92
9	52.95	11.08		23.72				87.75
10	11.36	19.33		7.57	17.78		42.38	98.42
11	57.84	1.25		30.33	2.00		18.00	109.42
12	47.58	17.83		28.92	.58		6.08	101.00
13	34.33	13.08		40.25	22.08			109.75
14	61.25	1.83			2.00	9.00	2.50	76.58
15	31.21	9.03		21.25	2.88			64.37
16	34.01	12.08	2.75	10.67	18.16	4.00	4.50	86.17
17	67.92	2.17	3.25	12.50	13.33	7.00		106.17
18	66.58	3.17		.50	2.42		9.25	81.92
19	48.28			19.95	18.20			86.42
20	23.20	48.70					7.25	79.15
Group means for the day	41.36	9.43	.30	20.80	9.01	1.42	9.72	92.04

results for the teachers working in conventional classroom arrangements. The twenty teachers are numbered in the first column in the table. The minutes per day that each teacher spent in total instruction are given in the last column of the table. The other columns break down the total daily instructional time of teachers into curriculum components for language arts, math, art, and other residual instruction. Furthermore, the classwide or small group-individual student basis of all curriculum instruction is designated where columns divide each of the curriculum areas for interaction bases of teacher and students.

The rows of the table, therefore, summarize the daily instructional activity for each teacher, and the bottom row of the table records the mean minutes expended per day in instruction for the entire group of teachers. For example, focusing on individual teachers, the table indicates that Teacher 1 spent 102 minutes of the 300 minute-5 hour classroom day in instruction. Of this total instructional time, 20.58 minutes were spent in individual-small group language arts teaching, 8 minutes were allocated to math instruction in individual-small group settings, and so on. The sum of these components of instruction for the day is 102 and a fraction minutes.

Two singular features about the results should be pointed out first. One of these is that the group mean time for total daily instruction, at the bottom of the last column, is a fraction over 90 minutes. This means that the group average time expended for daily instruction was 1½ hours in the 5 hours of the day that classes were scheduled. On the face of it, this appears to be a very small proportion of the total daily available time for instruction expended for this purpose. One reaction to this low total of daily instruction time might be to suspect that our definition of instruction was defined too narrowly to permit observers to identify all daily teaching that occurred.

In fact, however, the coding criteria defined instruction very broadly and, if anything, the result probably was that any coding errors were in the direction of coding too liberally for instruction. For example, because we were apprehensive about being able to accurately distinguish between some instruction and nonlearning activities, coders were instructed to code for instruction whenever teachers were reading to classes. Teachers often read to children as a form of "taking a break." However, if the story subject matter in any way appeared to teach indirectly by objects of exposition, the event was coded as instruction minutes of activity.

The second striking aspect of the results in the table is the extreme variance in the total daily instructional time between teachers. Teacher 6, for instance, accomplished just 48 minutes of instruction in the day. At the other extreme, Teacher 3 worked 141 minutes in instruction activity in a work day of equally long duration. Review of the entire table shows that the range and dispersion around the average of 92 daily minutes is indeed extensive. Teachers at the upper end of the range much exceeded 100 minutes of instruction per day, while at the opposite extreme, others were observed to expend as low as 40 to 50 minutes daily.

There is no ready explanation for this range of teaching time among teachers, but the diversity appears to be more related to individual idiosyncrasies of teaching methods and work pacing, and less related to influences of school program features. Concerning the latter, we are sure that a very small number of teachers had lower instruction minute totals because their classes were interrupted by conferences on the days they were studied. However, these kinds of program interruptions were relatively few as all observers agreed, and affected results for few teachers. The codings taken for minutes expended in administrative affairs was a very small fraction of teacher daily time.

Moreover, analyses that were performed to examine relationships between personal characteristics of teachers, and daily time expended in instruction, indicated that there were no significant relationships between daily time expended and teacher age, experience, and similar variables. A number of regression equations were computed to test these relationships, but none of the coefficients or other regression results was significant. Because teacher-pupil ratios, class schedules, and other program features in school were relatively similar, and because personal characteristics appeared unrelated to the dispersion, our tendency is to conclude that individual teacher differences were largely related to unmeasured influences of idiosyncratic work habits and random influences affective on the day of observation.

The most significant result of this part of the work study, however, is the finding that the average daily time teachers in conventional class arrangements expended in instruction was a relatively small part of total daily class time. And the principal reason this average time was so relatively low is that teachers in the conventional division of labor spent a large part of the school day in routine work and other noninstructional tasks. The work study results for total daily activities will make this quite clear.

Curriculum Component Instruction

The work study results for instruction can be organized to provide a detailed review of the curriculum areas to which teachers allocated daily teaching. The kind of teacher-class interaction that occurred in the curriculum teaching is also identifiable. Consequently, a very detailed perspective of events that occurred in instruction is obtainable. These results are reported in columns 2 to 8 in Table 3-1.

The information in those columns demonstrates that teachers gave first priority to instruction in the language arts of reading and writing. The group mean figures at the bottom of column 2 show that 41 minutes of their daily average of 92 instructional minutes were given over to individual-small group, language arts instruction. An additional 20-minute average instruction in this curriculum area was given on a classwide interaction basis as column 5 records. In total, therefore, almost 62 of the 92 minutes of daily instruction average time was devoted to language arts.

The detailed figures for individual teachers show the same magnitudes of dispersion around the group mean that were observed in the overall data for daily instruction time. However, the differences between teacher language art times are even more complex. A majority of teachers allocated most of their time to individual-small group teaching, but some spent most of their time on a classwide basis. This heavy allocation of work to language arts might be expected in elementary grades where children acquire basic language skills. A study product that is equally interesting is what the data reveal about teacher allocation of their remaining instruction time to other curriculum areas.

As a general proposition, the results show that instruction in math and numbers took a decidedly secondary place to reading and writing, while very little instruction was given in other areas. The group means for columns 3 and 6, at the bottom of those columns, show this directly. Those means of times for math indicate teachers averaged 9 daily minutes in both individual-small group and classwide math instruction. This totals to an average 18 daily minutes in all math instruction, or about one-fifth of the 92 average minutes spent in all daily instruction.

Taken altogether, the total information about curriculum instructional areas in the table reveals that instruction in an elementary curriculum is almost totally devoted to language skills, with a fraction of time allocated to math and numbers. When the study was being designed, we had some expectations that other subject matter areas would claim some larger proportion of total teaching time. The results show this is not the case. Only a fraction of time was given over to art, amounts so small that there are only traces in the records. And the total of instruction in history, geography, or other areas that was observed are included in the mere 9.7 minutes of average daily time in the "other" instruction column.

Persons who feel partial, and favor art or other subject matter areas for inclusion in curricula, will find disappointing surprises in these results. And those who believe the schools could do more to foster instruction in numerical skills will surely ponder what it means if teachers distribute less than 20 minutes per day of numerical instruction to classes of 20 to 30 students. For our part, the most surprising result of the study of teachers working in conventional arrangements was the basic finding that so relatively little time, an average 92 minutes, was spent in instruction of any kind.

Daily Instruction per Student

The finding that teachers produce relatively little instruction time as a part of daily class time leads to a number of interesting questions. One of these concerns the nature of individual attention children receive if instruction occupies a minority of class time. The matter has significance for the cost effectiveness objectives of the study. If the conventional teaching division of labor produces relatively little individual instruction, we shall want to compare this result with similar data from the work studies of teachers and paraprofessionals.

We have indicated that teachers and not students were the focus of observations for the work study. Consequently, we do not have direct observations that tell how much individual instruction children received. However, we can come very close to answering that question by inference from the teacher-student interaction data gathered in the study. With some interpolation, but little risk of error, these observations provide very interesting results.

In fact, the results reveal that a child received so little individual attention per day that the total of this attention surely did not average more than 1 or 2 minutes daily. We draw this conclusion from the data of Table 3-1 where it is indicated that the 20 teachers averaged 41 daily minutes in individual-small group language instruction, and just over 9 minutes in math instruction in the same interaction basis. This totals to just more than 50 minutes per day of individual-small group instruction in all subjects. Given that teacher-pupil ratios in these classes were approximately 1 teacher to 25 students, a realistic estimate of the direct attention an average child would receive daily can be made by dividing the 25-student figure into the 50-minute figure for daily, average, individual-small group instruction. The result indicates the average time per day is 2 minutes—a remarkably small proportion of the time per day that children are in school.

However, even this figure is too high an estimate for individual instruction received by children. The 50-minute figure included small group instruction as well as individual instruction. We are left, after this estimation process, with the knowledge that when allowance is made for small group instruction, individual attention per child is surely much less than a 2-minute average per day. No data is available that gives variances around the average figures. But with such a low average, one can assume few children would get significantly more individual attention.

These findings about instruction per child have special significance in the context of this study. Individual instruction is accorded special value in many educational contexts, but it is particularly prized in programs of compensatory education. The purposes of these programs are to redress low educational achievement. A presumption is that relatively low educational achievement cannot be brought up to standard unless special, tutorial teaching with large components of individual attention is offered children. These findings about teacher-child interaction have special relevance, therefore, because this cost effectiveness study was performed in the context of a compensatory educational program. These results will later be compared to results in the same category for paraprofessionals and for teachers who worked with their assistance.

We had no preconceptions when the study was being performed about the amount of instruction teachers produced. In fact, no information existed from which preconceptions might arise. When the results were accumulated, we found that persons who saw the data were uniformly surprised at what they considered to be the low proportion of daily time given to instruction. Most persons who were asked to estimate what amount of teacher time would daily be given to instruction almost always guessed, without knowing study results, that approximately one-half or more of daily work time would be spent in instruction activities.

Is it possible that the twenty teacher subjects in our group were somehow not representative, or were their work situations unique in ways that curtailed instructional opportunities? There are several reasons why we are sure this is not the case. First, as later chapters detail, the same general magnitudes of results were obtained in studies of other teacher populations. In addition, the teachers in this group worked in classes and schools that were not unusual for their curricula, daily schedules, and routines. More important, information from the work study that indicates how teachers spent the remainder of their daily work time shows why relatively little time was available for instruction. This information confirms the contentions of teachers who indicate that the organization of their work gives them little time to teach.

Daily Distribution of All Work

If instruction activities occupy relatively little of the teachers' work days, what are the other activities that they engage in daily? The information in Table 3-2 has been arranged to answer this question. The first column lists the hours of the school day when children attended classes. The rows corresponding to each hour show the average number of minutes in each hour that the teacher group expended in all the work categories defined for the study. The "Other" column

Table 3-2
Distribution of Daily Work within Hours of the Day, and by Work Categories, Twenty Teachers Working Conventionally

Hour of Class Day	Minutes of Instruction*	Minutes of Routine	Minutes of Nonlearning	Minutes of Other	Minutes of Out
9:00-10:00	19.2	26.5	13.0	1.1	.3
10:00-11:00	26.1	25.0	5.8	.4	2.7
11:00-12:00	10.6	19.5	2.7	.9	26.3
12:00-1:00	13.1	21.4	5.7	1.5	18.3
1:00-2:00	17.5	30.7	7.9	1.6	2.3
2:00-2:30	5.6	20.6	3.8	0.0	0.0
Group means for the day	92.0	143.7	38.9	5.5	49.9

*Column totals may not add to 60 minutes exactly because of rounding.

is a composite column where the hourly average times for planning, evaluation, administration, aide, and inactive have been pooled together for each hour. Totals for day averages are listed in the table bottom row. With this information, therefore, it is possible to inspect teachers' average activity times by hour of the day and for the entire day.

The information in the second table column shows that in each hour of the class day instruction seldom took up as much as 30 percent of the hour. Usually it was less than that. Only in the second hour of the day did instruction take as much as 43 percent of that hour, or a mean 26 minutes out of 60. In the hours after 11:00 A.M., there was only one where much instruction was performed at all: 17 minutes in the second hour of the afternoon. What is discernible in the hourly distribution of instruction is an apparent "warm up" and peak of instruction that occurs in the first two hours of the morning. After that it would appear that midday break schedules and, perhaps, fatigue cycles diminish amounts of instruction. The day totals indicate that 92 minutes or 28 percent of all minutes in the class meeting day were spent in instruction.

The general hour-by-hour pattern of activities recorded in the table confirms what we thought we discerned in class observation work before results were totaled and assembled. There was typically an early day takeoff into more concentrated instruction when students and teachers were fresh. This was followed by midday declines in part linked to occurrence of the midday break schedule. Afternoons were times when relatively little instruction was accomplished, except in the minutes right after class meetings started. Our data have captured and generalized this diurnal cycle.

School break schedules and apparent rest-fatigue cycles explain some of the variance in hourly instruction observed. However, the very organization of teachers' work in the conventional single teacher system accounts for more variance. Throughout the hours of the day teacher time devoted to routine work was a much greater proportion of time than was instructional time. Comparison of hourly average times for instruction and routine work shows that time expended in routine was usually close to double or more of the percentage of hourly instruction time. In only one hour of the day, the 10:00 to 11:00 A.M. hour, did average time for instruction work exceed the average of teachers' routine work time. And this large amount of routine work is also reflected in daily totals that indicate 143 minutes, or 43 percent of daily time, was spent in routine work while 28 percent of time was expended in instruction.

With these results the work study established that routine work, as we defined it, is the major category of work in which teachers spend their time. The definition of routine was established principally on the standard that work so classified could be done by nonprofessionals. The particulars of the definition included all housekeeping, material handling, clerical, and other tasks that required no professional training or judgment. The results of the work study reveal that advocates of teacher specialization are correct where they assume work days of teachers are much taken up with nonprofessional work. The results indicate the conventional teaching division of tasks offers nonprofessionals much to do.

Teachers' time allocated to other categories of the work study—nonlearning, planning, evaluation, administration, and inactive—proved to occupy a very small part of teacher work days. The averages in the table show this quite clearly. One thing that is apparent from review of these categories is that classrooms are busy places where relatively little time is lost because leisure is consumed in classes. The nonlearning and inactive category average times were a very small proportion of time in the school day.

So little work time was coded in these categories that at first we thought something was amiss. Close checks, however, proved that coding was reliable. There simply proved to be very little work performed by teachers in these categories during the school day hours when children were in school. Planning and evaluation work, as we learned from the study and testimony of teachers, was almost always performed in hours before and after classes, or at home at night. According to teacher testimony, but not any observations we made, these outside school work activities occupied their time for an average one and one-half hours daily.

The conventional teaching division of work in the lower grades imposes such a variety of tasks on teachers that only about one fourth of the time they spend in classroom work is devoted to instruction, broadly defined. Nearly one half of the time in teacher work days is taken up with routine work that requires no professional training or skills. Most teachers place great value on instruction that is given in more tutorial sessions with individual students or small class groups. However, the system in which they work allows them to average something less than two minutes of individual attention per day per child.

The relatively low proportion of time spent in all instruction cannot be attributed to teacher deficiencies. In this work system, teachers are busily occupied throughout the school day with the mixture of professional and nonprofessional tasks the system imposes. The findings of this first part of the work study support the viewpoint of educators and others who believe conventional work arrangements could be modified to specialize the teaching division of labor, and provide teachers with more exclusively professional work. In Chapter 4, work study results are reported for teaching positions for which modifications were attempted.

4

Teacher Work in the New Division of Labor

The work study results for teachers working in conventional assignments indicate why school administrators might elect to change that division of labor. But will new arrangements, including paraprofessionals, necessarily permit teachers to specialize more effectively in professional, instructional tasks? In this chapter, work study data for teachers who worked with paraprofessionals is reviewed and compared with the data for teachers who worked in conventional assignments. The questions of special interest are as follows: Did more specialization occur in work, as measured by increased production of instruction and decreases in work time devoted to nonprofessional, routine, tasks? Moreover, did the new work division change the nature of student and teacher interaction so more individualized teaching was performed? The results from the study of twenty-seven Portland teachers who were teamed with paraprofessionals answer these questions quite clearly.

Teachers who worked with paraprofessionals differed very little in terms of personal and occupational backgrounds from the teachers who worked in traditional arrangements. In average terms, they were only slightly younger and less experienced. The fundamental difference in their work environments was that they taught classes largely made up of black children in the Area I compensatory education program. Teaming with paraprofessionals was arranged so that each teacher had the services of one paraprofessional available for one half of each school day. The school district management had explicitly counseled school staff that paraprofessionals were employed for the purpose of assisting teachers in instruction and relieving them of routine work. Teachers were instructed to use the services of paraprofessionals, in addition, to increase the instruction that both staff members could make available to children.

Comparative Production of Instruction

The information in Table 4-1 summarizes work study instruction observations for the twenty-seven teachers who were teamed with paraprofessionals. To facilitate comparisons, the bottom table row with the heading "Group Means for The Day" includes means for both teacher groups, with brackets placed around the means, brought over from Table 3-1, for teachers who worked in conventional positions. The most interesting aspect of the figures in the table is that the magnitudes of the instruction time averages are not very different from the times reported in Table 3-1 for teachers working conventionally.

41

Table 4-1
Daily Minutes Expended in Instruction Time (IN) and Curriculum Subcategories of IN, Including Class Interaction Basis, Twenty-Seven Teachers with Paraprofessionals

Teacher Number	Teacher Daily Minutes of Individual and Small Group Language Arts Instruction	Teacher Daily Minutes of Individual and Small Group Math Instruction	Teacher Daily Minutes of Individual and Small Group Art Instruction	Teacher Daily Minutes of Classwide Language Arts Instruction	Teacher Daily Minutes of Classwide Math Instruction	Teacher Daily Minutes of Classwide Art Instruction	Other	Teacher Total Daily Instructional Time
1	31.25		.67	10.17		7.25		49.33
2	67.78			47.23	4.35		6.40	125.77
3	128.40	1.08						129.48
4	1.33			50.30	9.15			60.78
5	32.50	51.75		1.83				86.08
6	164.42			.73				165.15
7	33.06	20.38		30.29	5.24			88.97
8	21.63	27.47	11.33	47.67		6.83		114.93
9	70.13	.25		31.58		20.92		122.88
10	17.24			31.81				49.05
11	60.45			15.73		1.87		78.05
12	74.61	29.72		42.59				146.92
13	50.02	56.75		26.38		16.83	19.67	169.65

14	62.43	23.55		27.70	25.17	11.00		149.85
15	41.91	11.42		14.50		18.75		86.58
16	32.95		13.12	71.08		9.25		126.40
17	73.41	3.00		48.92		4.50		129.83
18	32.95	22.40		79.10				134.45
19	21.07	27.27		12.74				61.08
20	55.59	21.15		56.28				133.02
21	47.35	26.73		17.75	2.72	23.88	2.42	120.85
22	94.06	5.35		23.01	15.58			138.00
23	41.54			19.88				61.42
24	40.08	8.42		62.27	7.50	13.95		132.22
25	43.78	.75		31.36	4.86			80.75
26	82.58	9.85		39.05	23.42			154.90
27	2.84	21.83		8.91	20.07		.75	54.40
Group means for the day	52.79	13.67	.93	31.44	4.37	5.00	1.08	109.29
Group means for the day Conventional Teachers (from Table 3-1)	(41.36)	(9.43)	(.30)	(20.80)	(9.01)	(1.42)	(9.72)	(92.04)

As the mean times in the bottom row show, the average daily teacher minutes committed to instruction were 109 minutes for the teachers who worked with paraprofessionals. This figure exceeds the 92 average minutes for teachers working conventionally. This difference of 17 minutes daily is certainly not substantial, however, unless one wishes to consider that any moderate increase in daily instruction time is a valuable improvement over the relatively little daily instruction produced in conventional work arrangements.

The individual teacher work times in the rows reveal the same degrees of broad dispersion around the group 109-minute average figure as was evident in the times for teachers working conventionally. In this second teacher group also, some teachers produced as low as 40 to 50 daily instruction minutes. Others at the upper distribution points worked 150 to 160 minutes in daily instruction. In absolute terms, these are differences of nearly three fourths of an hour and 3 hours between higher and lower producers in the range. If anything, this range for teachers working with paraprofessionals displays somewhat greater dispersion than the range for the other teacher group. The proportion of teachers who worked with paraprofessionals that worked more than 100 minutes in daily instruction is greater than the proportion who worked conventionally and exceeded 100 minutes.

These work time dispersions and average time data appear to indicate that teachers who worked in the new system produced moderately more instruction. However, statistical testing does not support the conclusion that there are significant differences between the two teacher groups' average daily instructional times. To test these averages for significance of differences, a one-way analysis of variance was computed. The test data and results are given in Table 4-2. The F statistic 3.18 is not significant, indicating that the hypothesis of no significant

Table 4-2
One-Way Analysis of Variance of Mean Daily Minutes Expended in Instruction, Teachers Working with and without Paraprofessionals (Twenty-Seven with Paraprofessionals, Twenty Working Conventionally)

	Instructional Minutes
Teachers with paraprofessionals	
Mean minutes daily	109.28
S.D.	37.54
Teachers working conventionally	
Mean minutes daily	92.04
S.D.	24.79
Total sample	
Mean minutes daily	101.94
S.D.	33.54
Between variance	3418.00
Within variance	1074.11
F RATIO	3.18

differences is confirmed. The work study data for average daily instructional time, therefore, do not indicate that the teachers' daily production of instruction was much affected by teaming with paraprofessionals.

Comparative Instruction in Curriculum Components

The daily average times both groups expended in instruction were not significantly different, but this result could have occurred while instruction in curriculum components differed within those averages. What do the results indicate about the comparative amounts of instruction the two teacher groups expended in language arts, math, and other curriculum areas?

Focusing on the group means for daily instruction at the bottom of Table 4-1, the means for daily minutes of language arts, math, and other instruction by the teacher show that those who worked with paraprofessionals spent moderately more time in individual-small group instruction in both language arts and in math. Their average minutes for language arts instruction on this pupil interaction basis was 52 minutes compared to 41 minutes for teachers working without paraprofessionals. They also worked more on this interaction basis in math, but not much more; math took a decided second place in teacher attention to language arts. The total amounts of time expended for instruction in art and other remaining areas was a trivial part of the teaching day, very much like the results for teachers who worked in conventional assignments.

If there is one striking feature about the overall results in Table 4-1, it is that they are, in general, so much like the results in Table 3-1 for teachers working conventionally. Not only are the average times for specific columns relatively alike in general magnitude but the totals are consistent where they reveal that the teacher groups averaged roughly the same proportions of daily time in curriculum areas. The data from both tables make it apparent that language arts is the core of the elementary school curriculum, with math-numerical instruction decidedly second best as the only other real claimant on teacher time. Both teacher groups averaged just over 18 minutes of total classwide plus individual-small group math instruction per day. No other curriculum areas received significant attention.

Comparative Daily Instruction per Student

An important goal the school district sought to achieve when paraprofessional assistants were assigned to teachers was provision of more individualized, remedial, instruction for the disadvantaged children in the compensatory education program. This objective may have been achieved through the joint teaching inputs of both teachers and paraprofessionals. This is a question considered in the next chapter. Here the concern is to determine if teachers working with paraprofessionals produced more individualized instruction when the new work division was introduced.

The answer to this question is that teachers teamed with paraprofessionals produced slightly more individual-small group instruction as measured by their daily averages. But the differences are so slight, it is difficult to assign much importance to them. Table 4-1 shows that they averaged 11 minutes more daily of language arts instruction, and 4 minutes more of math instruction in the more individualized interaction bases. In percentage terms, teachers in the new system totaled an average 67 of their 109 daily instruction minutes, or 60 percent of that time, in closer instructional interaction. The percentage for teachers working alone was 55 percent.

However, it is more meaningful to consider if relatively minor differences like these could have importance for instruction of children. Considered from this standpoint, the answer must be that a child in a class of twenty-five is not likely to have different experiences daily because a teacher commits one or a fraction more minutes to individual instruction.

Comparative Distribution of All
Daily Work Time

A school district objective in specializing the professional division of labor by employing paraprofessionals was to reduce the nonprofessional routine work professionals perform. Little of the study evidence so far reviewed indicates that teachers instructed significantly more when paraprofessionals were assisting them. But was the parallel goal of reducing teacher routine work achieved? The work study observations for routine and the other categories that occupied the work day answer this question.

The information in Table 4-3 summarizes the total daily work data for both teacher groups by the hours of the class day and, in the bottom "Day Total" row, for the entire day. The column for the "Routine Work" category shows that, hour by hour, the number of minutes both groups expended on routine work was very similar. There are moderate differences in the first and last hours of the day, but even these differences are unimportant in the context of the total daily average. What is more significant and interesting is that in the hours from 10 A.M. to 2 P.M., the average hourly time spent in routine by the groups did not differ by more than three minutes in any hour. Results of this sort indicate that the work tasks of both teacher groups were homogeneous. The comparability of the results also is an excellent indication that the observation system produced results of high reliability for group averages.

The similarities in the results for routine work indicate that teaming teachers

Table 4-3

Average Minutes Expended in the Activity Categories by the Hours of the Day, and for the Total Day, Teachers with and Without Paraprofessionals (Teachers with Paraprofessionals N=27) (Teachers without Paraprofessionals N=20)

Hours	Activity Categories	Instruction (IN)*		Routine Work (ROUT)		Nonlearning (NONL)		Other	
		Min.	%	Min.	%	Min.	%	Min.	%
9:00-10:00	Teachers with paraprofessionals	26.5	44.2	18.9	31.5	9.8	16.3	3.0	5.0
	Teachers without paraprofessionals	19.2	31.9	26.5	44.2	13.0	21.6	1.1	1.8
10:00-11:00	Teachers with paraprofessionals	24.3	40.5	23.1	38.5	7.2	12.1	2.3	3.9
	Teachers without paraprofessionals	26.1	43.5	25.0	41.7	5.8	9.7	0.4	0.6
11:00-12:00	Teachers with paraprofessionals	19.1	31.8	19.7	32.8	2.8	4.7	2.3	3.8
	Teachers without paraprofessionals	10.6	17.6	19.5	32.5	2.7	4.5	0.9	1.4
12:00-1:00	Teachers with paraprofessionals	11.4	19.0	18.3	30.5	4.5	7.5	2.0	3.4
	Teachers without paraprofessionals	13.1	21.9	21.4	35.6	5.7	9.5	1.5	2.6
1:00-2:00	Teachers with paraprofessionals	19.8	33.1	32.0	53.3	4.4	7.3	1.9	3.2
	Teachers without paraprofessionals	17.5	29.2	30.7	51.1	7.9	13.2	1.6	2.6
2:00-3:00	Teachers with paraprofessionals	8.3	27.3	15.4	51.2	3.0	9.9	2.3	7.8
	Teachers without paraprofessionals	5.6	18.6	20.6	68.6	3.8	12.6	0.0	0.1
Day Totals	Teachers with paraprofessionals	109.3	33.1	127.3	38.6	31.7	9.6	13.9	4.2
	Teachers without paraprofessionals	92.0	27.9	143.7	43.5	38.9	11.8	5.5	1.7

*Row totals may not add to exactly 60 minutes, or 100 percent because of rounding.

with paraprofessionals, as it was done in Portland, did not significantly reduce the routine, nonprofessional tasks teachers performed. The figures in the table for the observation categories Nonlearning, Other, and Out show somewhat more variance hour by hour. However, the group averages for the day totals are again quite similar. The average minutes daily expended by both groups in nonlearning activities differ by only two percentage points. The minutes in the "Out" category, which are largely a reflection of uniform district free time scheduling, are all but identical.

All of the observations for planning, evaluation, administration, inactive, and aide proved to identify such a small proportion of teacher daily time that they were pooled in the "Other" category. Even when the minutes for all these categories are so pooled, the total daily minutes registered in "Other" are remarkably low. We noted earlier that planning and evaluation activities proved to be performed outside of class meeting hours, and this fact partially explains the low total. However, in planning the work study we took a clue from critics of bureaucratic tendencies. Our expectation, therefore, was that administration activities might well impinge on some moderate part of teacher class days. However, the very few observations made for the category "Administration" indicate that managers of schools must certainly avoid scheduling administrative tasks for teachers during class hours.

The category Aide was also included in the Other category. Another expectation we had was that, in the work division between teachers and paraprofessionals, moderate amounts of daily time would be spent in consultations and other work-related interaction. However, to a surprising extent we found that teachers and paraprofessionals expended only fractions of minutes in interaction in the time of the day that children were in classes. On questioning staff, we learned that most consultations occurred before and after classes, and during the free time in the day. Again, this is more evidence that classrooms are such busy places during the time children are in school that there is little time for interstaff consultations or unscheduled interactions. More relevant for study purposes, the very few Aide observations suggest that time expended in teacher-paraprofessional interaction did not curtail instructional opportunities.

To this point, our conclusion has been that there were no important differences in the times the teacher groups expended in noninstructional activities. This conclusion has been based on direct inspection of summary data. Tables 4-4 and 4-5 compare the hourly and total day activities of the two teacher groups. The observation data averages have been arranged to show the average minutes expended by the hours in the several categories. For example, for the first daily hour shown in Table 4-4, all the category mean times for the two groups are listed for that hour. The sum of the averages for each group, obtained by adding the average minutes in the columns, equals one hour. The last entry in Table 4-5 arranges data in the same fashion, but for the total day averages for the groups. Each of the separate hourly summaries within the larger tables are subtables designed for chi-square tests.

Table 4-4

Comparison of Minutes Expended in the Activity Categories, in the Morning, Including Chi-Square Tests for Significance of Differences, Teachers with and without Paraprofessionals (Teachers with paraprofessionals N=27) (Teachers without Paraprofessionals N=20)

9:00-10:00	Minutes for Teachers with Paraprofessionals*	Minutes for Teachers without Paraprofessionals
IN	26.5	19.2
ROUT	18.9	26.5
NONL	9.8	13.0
OUT	1.8	0.3
OTHER	3.0	1.1
Yates Chi-Square is: D.F.: 4	2.39 (N.S.)	

10:00-11:00	Minutes for Teachers with Paraprofessionals	Minutes for Teachers without Paraprofessionals
IN	24.3	26.1
ROUT	23.1	25.0
NONL	7.2	5.8
OUT	3.1	2.7
OTHER	2.3	0.4
Yates Chi-Square is: D.F.: 4	0.43 (N.S.)	

11:00-12:00	Minutes for Teachers with Paraprofessionals	Minutes for Teachers without Paraprofessionals
IN	19.1	10.6
ROUT	19.7	19.5
NONL	2.8	2.7
OUT	16.2	26.3
OTHER	2.3	0.9
Yates Chi-Square is: D.F.: 4	4.05 (Sig. .03)	

*Column Totals may not add to 60 minutes because of rounding.

The chi-square tests are used to determine the significance of differences for the average minutes the two teacher groups expended in the several activity categories for each hour of the day. The tests specifically are for the null hypothesis that there is no significant difference in the relative amount of minutes per day (or per total day) the two groups expended in the categories observed. The data and tests may be reviewed beginning with the earliest 9:00 to 10:00 A.M. hour of the work day.

That hour is the one, visual inspection suggests, that registers the largest, if

Table 4-5

Comparison of Minutes Expended in the Activity Categories, in the Afternoon, and Totals for the Day, Including Chi-Square Tests for Significance of Differences, Teachers with and without Paraprofessionals (Teachers with Paraprofessionals N = 27) (Teachers without Paraprofessionals N = 20)

12:00-1:00	Minutes for Teachers with Paraprofessionals	Minutes for Teachers without Paraprofessionals
IN	11.4	13.1
ROUT	18.3	21.4
NONL	4.5	5.7
OUT	23.8	18.3
OTHER	2.0	1.5
Yates Chi-Square is: D.F.: 4	0.69 (N.S.)	

1:00-2:00	Minutes for Teachers with Paraprofessionals	Minutes for Teachers Without Paraprofessionals
IN	19.8	17.5
ROUT	32.0	30.7
NONL	4.4	7.9
OUT	1.9	2.3
OTHER	1.9	1.6
Yates Chi-Square is: D.F.: 4	0.78 (N.S.)	

2:00-3:00	Minutes for Teachers with Paraprofessionals	Minutes for Teachers without Paraprofessionals
IN	8.3	5.6
ROUT	15.4	20.6
NONL	3.0	3.8
OUT	1.1	0.0
OTHER	2.3	0.0
Yates Chi-Square is: D.F.: 4	1.42 (N.S.)	

Totals for day	Minutes for Teachers with Paraprofessionals	Minutes for Teachers without Paraprofessionals
IN	109.3	92.0
ROUT	127.3	143.7
NONL	31.7	38.9
OUT	47.9	49.9
OTHER	13.9	5.5
Yates Chi-Square is: D.F.: 4	5.61 (Sig. .02)	

*Column totals may not add to 60 minutes because of rounding.

moderate, differences between the two groups' hourly averages for instruction and routine work. In the observation process, observers were sure teachers teamed with paraprofessionals were able to teach more in that hour, principally because paraprofessionals usually assisted teachers by collecting lunch money and by performing other representative early day tasks. The chi-square test, however, confirms the null hypothesis of no significant difference in average times expended within the categories for teachers with and without professionals. One cannot conclude that a redistribution of teacher time occurred in this hour of the day because of teacher teaming with paraprofessionals.

As the data for the 10:00 to 11:00 hour indicate, this hour is an important teaching hour in the day. Both teacher groups expended almost as much instruction in this hour as they did in any other daily hour. The average activity times for all categories are quite similar for both teacher groups. The chi-square test reflects this relative homogeneity. The test result is not significant.

The hour 11:00 to 12:00 shows a decline in both instruction and routine activities, and an increase in Out average time, as the lunch hour begins to impinge upon classroom activities. The average times for teachers with paraprofessionals for instruction show that they taught moderately more in this hour, and were Out much less than teachers working without paraprofessionals. During observation days observers noted that teachers working in conventional arrangements had to expend more time getting children ready for class passing and lunch during the late minutes of this hour. In addition, teachers and paraprofessionals often scheduled their free time during this period so that one of them would remain with the children. This is the probable explanation for the greater instruction and reduced "Out" time for that teacher group. The chi-square test for this hour is significant at .03. The differences between the group category times were probably not a result of chance occurrences.

The observation study results for the afternoon hours and for the total day are reported in Table 4-5. In the noon hour, activities associated with lunch periods impinge on observation results. Instruction declines, "Out" time averages increase, and the results are generally similar for both teacher groups. The chi-square test of differences is not significant.

The same result obtains for the hours between 1:00 and 3:00 P.M. The activity times of both groups have average values that are quite similar, and the chi-square tests are not significant. The 2:00 to 3:00 hour is only a thirty-minute period because school ends for the day at the half hour.

The final data block in Table 4-5 is the most important one in the series. These average category times are for the full five and one-half hour day. The averages, therefore, summarize the daily distribution of thousands of separate observations that observers made for the categories. The day total accumulates observations that were gathered in more than 400 hours of observation time and consequently smooths out data disturbances due to daily schedules and other influences.

The data there show that teachers who were teamed with paraprofessionals exceeded the average instruction work of the other teacher group by some seventeen minutes daily. They also performed an average sixteen minutes less routine work daily, and had somewhat less nonlearning time. The chi-square test for the two groups indicates that the group differences were probably not random differences. The chi-square test for these work category time distributions for the full day are significant at the .02 level. The evidence, therefore, is that when paraprofessionals worked with teachers, the teachers' average daily work times in categories were expended in different proportions in comparison to the category time allocations of teachers without paraprofessionals.

The chi-square test confirms that teachers spent their daily work time somewhat differently when paraprofessionals were assigned to them. However, it is worthwhile to probe further the more general significance of this fact. Study results show that very minor differences in work were registered by the two groups during the hour-by-hour progress of the day. Also, analysis of variance results reported earlier indicated that when group average times for daily instruction were tested for significance of differences, the results were not significant. That negative finding does not contradict the chi-square results. The chi-square result was for a test of group differences for proportions of daily time allocated to all work categories. But apart from these probability test results, it is worthwhile to inquire if the daily work time differences between the groups might be important in any practical way.

Are these amounts of additional instruction and reduced routine work trivial or important as a part of the total, daily, work of teachers? It is possible to disagree about this question as a matter of judgment. The seventeen more minutes that teachers with paraprofessionals averaged in instruction is not a large proportion of the five-hour working day. On the other hand, considering that teachers working alone taught only an average of 92 minutes per day, 17 minutes might be considered a significant addition to that total.

Our conclusion on this matter is that the differences between the two groups were not great, not strongly confirmed by all statistical tests, and more important, they would have little importance in an instructional program context. It is difficult to believe that any important changes in the nature of instruction would result from differences of this degree.

Summary

The extensive data of the work study are rich with implications about the teaching processes in schools. Many persons who have had a preview of the work study data find relationships that are significant to their own interests. Often these relationships are quite secondary to the central focus of this study and cost effectiveness analysis. In these comments, we consider the findings that are more relevant to that focus. Subsequently, in the next chapter when reports of the work study are concluded, more general study implications are discussed.

The findings reported in this chapter support the conclusion that teachers did not specialize professionally and perform much more productive instructional work when paraprofessionals were teamed with them. Their involvement with nonprofessional routine work also did not decline importantly. The study results provide very tentative indications that modest additional amounts of instruction may have been performed, but these findings do not hold up well to statistical testing. More important, these minor observed shifts in work tasks were hardly large enough to influence the nature of instruction individual children received.

A finding that will interest many persons is the basic finding, for both teacher groups, that they performed so little instruction as a proportion of all daily work time. Even if one believes that children may not need much individual attention to learn well, or that they learn from peers as well as teachers, the amount of instruction children received appears to be remarkably small in given time periods. This situation is largely attributable to the fact that the amount of time teachers must spend on routine and other nonprofessional activities crowds out available instruction time.

The study information quite clearly established that the existing, conventional, division of labor was not changed in ways that permitted development of teacher specialization when paraprofessionals were employed. Teachers may have used the assistance of paraprofessionals in ways that were reasonably effective for obtaining productive work from paraprofessionals. This question is examined in Chapter 5, where results from study of paraprofessional work are reported. However, all information available indicates that the teamed teachers themselves performed in work substantially like teachers who work in conventional classroom work arrangements.

Normal teacher class participation patterns were essentially retained, as all the work study particulars imply, except that paraprofessionals were in the classrooms several hours a day. While the work category daily times for instruction and routine reveal this uniformity of work between the two teacher groups, the extremely little time that teachers spent in "Aide" activity is perhaps the most revealing aspect that demonstrates homogeneity of teacher work roles. It seems reasonable to expect that if teachers' work roles had changed at all fundamentally, teachers would have worked in new patterns of association with their paraprofessionals. However, observation data indicates that few teachers spent more than one or two daily classroom minutes in work interaction with paraprofessionals. This, and the more general pattern of study results, would indicate that a new division of labor for teachers was not achieved when paraprofessionals were assigned to work with them.

5 Paraprofessional Work and Work Study Conclusions

Arguments favorable to paraprofessional employment make several assumptions about the nature of professional work and the work capabilities of paraprofessionals. One assumption is that professional work is burdened with nonprofessional tasks. The information reported in the last two chapters confirms this assumption for the case of teachers in the lower grades. Another assumption is that persons with no professional training or experience can capably perform part of the work that professionals have historically performed. This assumption has never been tested by comprehensive observation and study. The information about paraprofessional work discussed in this chapter permits direct appraisal of this last assumption.

None of the twenty-eight paraprofessionals whose work was studied had educational backgrounds that prepared them for work in education. What training they received from the district was a minimum of on-the-job training given by their teacher co-workers. Most of them were married women, in their thirties, from lower and lower-middle class backgrounds. They averaged sixteen months of employment in the school district when the study was performed. Their mean educational attainment was just over thirteen years, indicating they were moderately well educated. However, few of them had much higher education, and none of them had anything like the professional preparation that is required of classroom teachers.[a]

The work assignment patterns developed in the schools for paraprofessionals were the result of general applications of district policies and, more specifically, the result of teacher choices and applications of district policies. That is, while the district administration had disseminated the policy that paraprofessionals were to be used to increase teaching contacts per child, teachers who worked with paraprofessionals were left with discretion to work out the practical implementation of this policy. The work observation data for paraprofessionals indicate what work task allocations teachers chose for their nonprofessional co-workers.

Production of Instruction by Paraprofessionals

One of the most unexpected results of the research was the work study finding concerning the total daily time paraprofessionals expended in instruction for

---

[a]Additional details concerning paraprofessionals' personal characteristics are given in Appendix B.

children. They worked split assignments between teachers and they were observed doing substantial routine work in classrooms. Nevertheless, the study results indicate paraprofessionals actually performed more instruction during the day than did the teachers who worked with them. Furthermore, the average amount of daily time paraprofessionals expended in instruction was also more than that of teachers who worked in conventional class arrangements. Paraprofessionals worked in instruction an average 128 minutes daily. The average daily figures for teachers who worked with and without paraprofessionals were 109 and 92 minutes, respectively. The assistants who were employed so that professional teachers might specialize and teach more, in fact, worked more like instructional specialists!

The information in Table 5-1 reports work study data for individuals and averages for the group.[b] In addition to the group daily instruction time average of 128 minutes, the results in the table are unusual in a number of other respects from similar information reported earlier for the two teacher groups. With regard to group dispersion of total daily minutes of instruction time, the range and dispersion around the group average 128 minutes is only superficially larger than ranges that were observed for teacher groups. Almost one half of the paraprofessionals had 150 or more instruction minutes daily, and the lower end of the range is only superficially extended to 16 minutes, a level where one isolated person registered. Many more paraprofessionals than teachers put in two or more hours of instruction daily.

The explanation for this result, where aides taught so much more daily, is not difficult to isolate. It is to be found in the patterns of paraprofessional utilization teachers evolved, each teacher making much the same, if independently made, choices with what proved to be remarkably similar work results. When teachers were assigned paraprofessionals, they were instructed to use them to increase instruction, as we have noted. However, nothing about the teachers' traditional work roles and responsibilities was deliberately altered or changed by any intervention processes from the organization. The previous chapter reported considerable information from which one can infer that teachers' work roles were very much unchanged despite paraprofessional teaming. This additional information about paraprofessional productivity in instruction tasks is, in fact, complimentary to that information about unchanged teacher roles. For when considered together, the total information reveals that paraprofessionals taught more, and teachers less, because teachers retained their traditional work patterns for housekeeping, child behavior monitoring, and other routine work, while paraprofessionals functioned in classes to specialize as remedial teachers during class hours. Paraprofessionals, therefore, were literally the specialized remedial teachers in the teams who had more opportunity to teach, while teachers

---

[b]Six of the twenty-eight paraprofessionals studied were part-time workers. Their less than full day work results are omitted from the table. However, on an hourly basis, these six had work results with averages nearly identical to the twenty-two full-time workers.

Table 5-1
Daily Minutes Expended in Instructional Time (IN) and Curriculum Subcategories of IN, Including Class Interaction Basis, Twenty-Two Paraprofessionals

Para. Number	Para. Daily Minutes of Individual and Small Group Language Arts Instruction	Para. Daily Minutes of Individual and Small Group Math Instruction	Para. Daily Minutes of Individual and Small Group Art Instruction	Para. Daily Minutes of Classwide Language Arts Instruction	Para. Daily Minutes of Classwide Math Instruction	Para. Daily Minutes of Classwide Art Instruction	Other	Paraprofessional Total Daily Instructional Instruction
1	32.30	44.80						77.10
2	187.83	9.84						197.67
3	133.17	1.33	34.33					168.83
4	119.93							119.93
5	16.63							16.63
6	25.08	8.87					17.38	51.33
7	65.50	75.00	5.50				33.00	179.00
8	110.30							110.30
9	44.25	18.27						62.52
10	175.73							175.73
11	74.24	13.28						87.52
12	86.40	32.50						118.90
13	122.71	28.17		6.50		21.25		178.63
14	18.43			42.11		15.27	43.59	119.40
15	65.93	12.70					.57	79.20
16	103.35			20.72				124.07
17	124.95	39.83	3.42					168.20
18	145.60							145.60
19	166.07							166.07
20	95.92	60.00						155.92
21	168.25							168.25
22	149.05	15.02						164.07
Group means for the day	101.44	16.35	1.96	3.15		1.66	4.29	128.86

continued their nonprofessional activities. This was not a planned or deliberate outcome, but rather one that naturally evolved in a situation where nothing specific suggested to teachers how they might change their work roles to actually accomplish specialization. The conclusion that the nonprofessionals were more like personnel who specialized is reinforced by the study information about the distribution of instruction in curriculum components.

Paraprofessional Instruction in
Curriculum Components

The results of curriculum area measurements of paraprofessional instruction demonstrate that they were almost entirely teaching specialists in language arts, or more specifically, reading. The heavy concentration of instruction time registered in the first column of Table 5-1 demonstrates this fact. The parapro-fessional mean daily time committed to individual-small group language arts instruction was 101 minutes. This figure is almost 80 percent of the total instruction time of 128 minutes they averaged daily. This is obviously a very desirable work contribution to a compensatory program that stressed develop-ment of basic, early, language skills.

The 101-minute average in this curriculum area is larger than the day average of instruction time in all curriculum areas for teachers who worked without paraprofessionals. And 101 minutes is almost double the amount of daily instruction in this language arts category that was averaged by teachers who were teamed with paraprofessionals. In a compensatory program where development of language skills had priority, paraprofessionals were the instructors who did most of the teaching in this priority area.

Turning to consider instruction in math, it is also notable that the daily mean time for paraprofessional instruction in math, on an individual small group basis, is also larger than the averages for the teacher groups. Paraprofessionals averaged 16 minutes daily. Teachers who worked with them averaged 13 minutes, and those working conventionally had even a lower daily math average of 9 minutes. Therefore, it is not quite correct to infer from the total data that paraprofession-als were primarily language arts instructors. Except that they did not teach math on a classwide basis, one could almost conclude that they taught more than teachers in both language arts and math—the two curriculum areas that all the data reveal are almost the entire elementary curriculum.

Paraprofessional Daily Instruction
per Student

One of the most singular features of the data in Table 5-1 is that the information there shows almost no entries in classwide instruction, and very large entries in the individual-small group columns. Taken altogether this result means that if children in a compensatory program class were going to receive any individual attention from an instructor, they would be about twice as likely to get that attention from a paraprofessional as from their teacher. This is merely a practical way to translate what the data show about the relative amounts of individual-small group instruction that teachers and paraprofessionals offered. More specifically, almost 120 of the paraprofessinals' daily average instruction minutes were expended in instruction on this more intimate interaction basis. By comparison, 67 of the teachers' 109 instructional minutes were so expended.

Nothing in the above comments should be taken to indicate that the instructional performance of teachers was somehow inferior to that of parapro-fessionals because of this relative allocation of time to children. Such an interpretation would be entirely incorrect because part of the reason these performances had these dimensions was because of deliberate choices of teachers. For example, teachers did not usually place entire classes in paraprofes-sionals' hands because they were not trained to teach this way, or teach with appropriate subject matter. The principal reason the results worked out as they did was that teachers often found it useful to have paraprofessionals do special tutoring with individuals or small groups while teachers then moved ahead faster with class instruction.

Paraprofessional production of individual-small group instruction had special secondary value, therefore, beyond its more immediate tutorial value. Employment of paraprofessionals in the division of labor not only more than doubled more tutorial opportunities for children; it also permitted teachers to make choices to distribute instructional treatments to entire classes or to persons and groups in ways they believed were more effective for educational ends.

**Daily Distribution of All
Paraprofessional Work**

If paraprofessionals produced more instruction than did teachers in a class day, then it might be expected that they also would produce less routine work in remaining portions of work days. This is just the result the observation study data measured. Table 5-2 brings together work study results for paraprofession-als and the two teacher groups, for the class hours of the day and for total class day results. Presented this way, the study data can be reviewed and comparisons made by minutes per hour, and in hourly percentage terms, for the work performed by all three groups.

The day total averages in the bottom table row show that paraprofessionals worked 128 minutes, or 39 percent of the daily minutes, in instruction. The data in the column for "Routine Work" indicate that they expended 118 or 35 percent of daily minutes in routine work. Both teacher groups spent more time per day in routine work. The teachers teamed with paraprofessionals spent 127

Table 5-2
Average Minutes Expended in Work Activity Categories by Hours of the Day and for the Total Day, Twenty-Eight Paraprofessionals, Twenty-Seven Teamed Teachers, and Twenty Teachers Working Conventionally

Activity Categories:		Instruction		Routine		Nonlearning		Other	
		Min.	%*	Min.	%	Min.	%	Min.	%
9:00-10:00	Paraprofessionals	25.4	42.3	22.9	38.2	3.0	5.0	5.0	8.4
	Teachers teamed	26.5	44.2	18.9	31.5	9.8	16.3	3.0	5.0
	Teachers conventional	19.2	31.9	26.5	44.2	13.0	21.6	1.1	1.8
10:00-11:00	Paraprofessionals	26.7	44.5	19.4	32.3	2.7	4.5	5.3	8.9
	Teachers teamed	24.3	40.5	23.1	38.5	7.2	12.1	2.3	3.9
	Teachers conventional	26.1	43.5	25.0	41.7	5.8	9.7	0.4	0.6
11:00-12:00	Paraprofessionals	20.7	34.6	24.4	40.7	2.0	3.3	2.1	3.5
	Teachers teamed	19.1	31.8	19.7	32.8	2.8	4.7	2.3	3.8
	Teachers conventional	10.6	17.6	19.5	32.5	2.7	4.5	0.9	1.4
12:00-1:00	Paraprofessionals	10.6	17.6	21.3	35.5	1.3	2.2	2.3	3.9
	Teachers teamed	11.4	19.0	18.3	30.5	4.5	7.5	2.0	3.4
	Teachers conventional	13.1	21.9	21.4	35.6	5.7	9.5	1.5	2.6
1:00-2:00	Paraprofessionals	32.8	54.6	17.5	29.1	2.1	3.5	5.1	8.4
	Teachers teamed	19.8	33.1	32.0	53.3	4.4	7.3	1.9	3.2
	Teachers conventional	17.5	29.2	30.7	51.1	7.9	13.2	1.6	2.6
2:00-2:30	Paraprofessionals	12.7	42.2	12.5	41.8	0.7	2.2	2.9	9.5
	Teachers teamed	8.3	27.3	15.4	51.2	3.0	9.9	2.3	7.8
	Teachers conventional	5.6	18.6	20.6	68.6	3.8	12.6	0.0	0.1
Day totals	Paraprofessionals	128.9	39.1	118.0	35.8	11.8	3.6	22.7	6.9
	Teachers teamed	109.3	33.1	127.3	38.6	31.7	9.6	13.9	4.2
	Teachers conventional	92.0	27.9	143.7	43.5	38.9	11.8	5.5	1.7

*Row percentages will not total 100 because minutes expended in Out category are omitted.

minutes, and teachers working conventionally spent much more time, 143 minutes, in work in this category. This work reversal, where nonprofessionals did less routine work than professionals, is another indication that paraprofessionals, contrary to expectations, were more specialized as instructors than were teachers.

The hour-by-hour allocations of work, which are reviewed in the hours from 9:00 to 2:30, show no distinctive patterns for the time expended by paraprofessionals in routine work. In some hours they did more and in other hours they did less routine work than did teachers. Only in the afternoon hours is a major difference apparent between their time expenditures. This difference is that from 1:00 on in the day, paraprofessionals expended much more time in instruction, and less in routine work, than did either teacher group. This result apparently happened because teachers could not as effectively organize their classes in P.M. hours for instruction as they could in morning hours. Paraprofessionals, for their part, continued right on in the P.M. hours of the day with individual-small group tutoring that was easier to control and direct into instructional consequences.

The lesser amount of time paraprofessionals spent in nonlearning activities and the greater amount in Other activities are also a reflection of the different class roles they performed. In every hour of the day, they registered significantly less time than did teachers in nonlearning activity, with the result that only fractions of the day were so taken up. Again, this result is atrributable to the fact that teachers were called upon for noninstructional discussions, to impose discipline, and perform other nonlearning tasks in classwide settings that consumed more time in this task category. Paraprofessionals, for their part, faced few of these distractions from instruction in their less than classwide teaching situations. The slightly more time paraprofessionals expended in Other activities was a consequence of their availability to function as messengers and jacks-of-all-trades.

Concerning the overall work results paraprofessionals accomplished, therefore, it is difficult not to be impressed with the amounts of instruction these relatively inexperienced and less educated persons contributed to the schools. Their instruction time per day exceeded the day totals of both teacher groups considerably. Moreover, the instruction they contributed was consistent with district goals for the compensatory program. Almost all their instruction was intensive tutorial language arts Instruction with individual children or small groups. A review of the records for production of instruction by both teachers and paraprofessionals suggests that, if paraprofessionals had not been hired, the disadvantaged children in the program would have received no exceptional degrees of instruction in the compensatory program.

Work Study Conclusions

The observations data of the work study provide the first comprehensive understanding of processes that occur in instructional and noninstructional teacher work. We concern ourselves, first, with summary comments that are relevant to the cost effectiveness purposes of the study. Later, remarks are offered about more general significance of the work study results. Presently, we reintroduce those questions of particular relevance to the cost-effectiveness study: Concerning teachers, did they achieve greater specialization in work so they could devote more time to teaching and less to routine tasks? Concerning paraprofessionals, did they relieve teachers of nonprofessional work and also contribute to a greater total of instruction for children? Did children receive more effective instructional treatments because teachers and paraprofessionals were newly teamed in the teaching division of labor?

The answers to these questions are relatively unambiguous in terms of what the work study data directly indicate. It is clear that teachers who worked with paraprofessionals did not achieve significantly greater specialization in instruction and related professional tasks. Nor did they perform less nonprofessional work to any important degree. In almost all respects their work results were quite comparable with the work of their peers who worked without the assistance of paraprofessionals. This study finding—in addition to much of what the social sciences have established about tendencies for human habits to persist—suggests that efficient specialization for teachers will not be achieved unless programs to change the teaching division of labor are deliberately designed to intervene and alter the structure of teacher work roles.

In this context, it is interesting to note that Portland teachers were encouraged by superiors to utilize paraprofessionals so that teachers could achieve greater specialization. Furthermore, teachers almost uniformly disliked the fact that their roles required so much performance of nonprofessional work. Also, there was little resistance to having paraprofessionals assigned within the work system. If anything, teachers who did not have aides assigned to them, or had them assigned for lesser parts of the work day, tended to feel this was an inequity. There is little evidence, therefore, that teachers worked the way they did because of "resistance to change."

However, despite encouragement and lack of resistance to change, teachers remained as "homeroom" class generalists. They received substantial help from paraprofessionals, but old conventional patterns of work performance persisted as teachers integrated their aides into classes to work parallel to the teachers' conventional roles. While teachers organized their teaching days in essentially conventional ways, paraprofessionals were used as ancillaries to those traditional patterns of work organization.

The amounts of professional and nonprofessional work teachers performed did not change, but it is possible that the quality of teachers' instruction may have been changed, in ways that we did not measure, because teachers were paired with paraprofessionals. Two factors suggest the possibility of these changes. One of these factors is the substantial reduction in staff-pupil ratios that occurred when paraprofessionals worked with teachers in classrooms. Where the usual teacher-pupil ratio in Portland schools was approximately one teacher to twenty-five children, this ratio was reduced by one half when teacher-paraprofessional teams were in classes and taught together. Also, it has been noted that teachers tended to use paraprofessionals to tutor children with special problems, while teachers then took opportunity to work, with less distraction, with the remaining children in classes. These facts indicate that teachers may have used the presence of paraprofessionals to make important changes affecting the quality of instruction even though the observation measurements did not record increases in the amounts of instruction teachers performed.

Another consequence of paraprofessional employment our measurements did not illuminate is any contribution paraprofessionals made to teaching effectiveness where they performed work for teachers during daily hours before and after classes. Paraprofessionals worked for teachers for one morning hour before classes met and for at least one hour after classes ended for the day. During these periods they did considerable work, some of which contributed to lesson plans and new patterns of enriched instruction. It is not apparent, however, that these work contributions of the teacher assistants curtailed the amount of routine work that teachers necessarily performed during the periods when classes met during the day.

For the research personnel who carried out the study, the most surprising general finding remains that teachers were still able to instruct for only a relatively small portion of the total class day. As we have indicated before, a teacher's nonprofessional activities have a way of crowding out available teaching time. This seems to be an inevitable process in a division of labor that uses professionals to perform so many housekeeping and other tasks that require little skill. Furthermore, there is irony here because many teachers would like to abandon this nonprofessional work, but our results show that it is difficult to change work behavior to accomplish this result as long as teachers are stationed in classrooms in customary ways.

These study results for teachers imply that teacher work roles, and the organizational modes that support these roles, will have to be significantly changed if the division of labor is to be redesigned to achieve more professional work. The results further suggest that changes in teacher work roles will have to divorce the professionals' instructional tasks from conventional class homeroom settings where considerable time is spent monitoring behavior of children, doing housekeeping, and other nonprofessional work. It seems almost certain, in fact, that if teachers are not taken out of their homeroom class roles and given greater opportunity to be full-time teaching specialists, then there will be few other ways to permit them to function as professionals.

Nothing the research team observed in many days of work in the schools indicated conclusively why it is necessary to assign professional teachers to homeroom classes. None of the tasks associated with the noninstructional tasks of a homeroom monitor require professional judgment. And everything we observed about the character and capabilities of paraprofessionals suggests that they could very successfully perform these roles. The homeroom monitor and housekeeping role requires maturity and good judgment, but professional task requirements are close to nil.

If there is one recommendation that emerges clearly for practical implementation from the work study, it is that schools experiment more with staff assignment plans that place paraprofessionals full time in the homeroom role while teachers function as full-time instructors who visit classes during the day primarily to teach. Staffing arrangements along these lines would instill a clear demarcation between instructional and noninstructional work, and make a clean break from conventional roles. Teachers would not necessarily be placed in an interaction status that is too remote from children because teachers would no longer work all day in "homerooms." In such a system, teachers could have more interaction, and more important interaction, as their instruction for children increased. Paraprofesionals, for their part, would function as monitors, prepare classes for teacher visitations, and also contribute additional instruction in the time they have remaining from more routine work. The general nature of the work study results clearly implies that if something like these new roles are not arranged in schools, professional work productivity of teachers will remain under the handicap of excessive nonprofessional tasks.

Concerning paraprofessionals, the results of this study are the first available that detail the substantial instructional contribution that nonprofessional staff can contribute to schools. Their teaching time per day exceeded the totals of both teacher groups considerably. Moreover, their instructional contribution was consistent with school district goals for the compensatory program. Almost all paraprofessional teaching was tutorial language arts instruction with individual children or small groups. The results clearly indicate that the children received considerably more attention when paraprofessionals were employed with teachers.

In a comparative context, the additional attention paraprofessionals gave to children takes on increased importance for a remedial program. The study findings reveal no teaching gains for teamed teachers, but in general, where the aides worked for two teachers and they contributed about one half of their two-hour average daily instruction to each class, then the twenty-four students in each class had much more opportunity for individual attention than they would have had with single teachers. The cost effectiveness implications of paraprofessional performance must be judged to be very favorable. Specific cost dimensions associated with this performance are the subject of the following chapter.

The implications of the new staffing system for students and their learning achievement cannot be fully assessed by noting only that they received more instructional attention. The evidence of the work study makes it quite obvious that individual attention is quite scarce in conventional classrooms and more than moderately increased when staff are teamed. The study data, therefore, permit the inference that individual children may improve in their learning achievement when the new staffing system is used. This, of course, is to posit a relationship between increased instructional attention and actual achievement that the work data did not directly assess. Chapter 8 of this volume reports analyses of children's reading achievement scores and addresses this question more fully.

In the introductory pages of this report, we noted that studies that have examined relationships between levels of school expenditure and student educational achievement have failed to find that the amount of expenditures is an important determinant of learning gains. In those pages, in addition, the author of the most important of these research studies was cited as suggesting that the reason for this finding may be that conventional modes of school organization may not mediate effectively between incremental money inputs and learning achievement. We raise this question for further discussion after reporting work study findings because the results support Professor Coleman's speculations about the ineffectiveness of school arrangements for the purposes described.

Instruction is by far the most expensive component of educational programs. It is in the area of instruction that most compensatory education programs have expended the largest amounts of exceptional funding in efforts to improve student achievement. And these expenditures would appear most defensible, for if student achievement is to be improved, it is tenable to assume it must be improved chiefly by changing the nature of instruction teachers can provide for children.

The results of this study, however, make it clear that teacher work roles are not structured so that exceptional inputs of school funds can affect the way that teachers instruct, interact with children, and allocate their time to professional and nonprofessional work. Merely raising teachers' salaries, providing more incentives, adding more teachers, or expending funds in similar ways will not change the fact that teachers can still teach only a small part of the school day and give little attention to individual children. In Portland, teachers worked with conscious efforts to try to raise the achievements of disadvantaged children in their classes. Even so, the only exceptional and new dimensions of instruction for children were provided by paraprofessionals. Teachers were unable to alter the work patterns of their traditional work roles. Children received exceptional instruction only from paraprofessionals whose employment costs were borne by new expenditures of local, state, and federal funds. Newer, more effective, instruction was purchased for children, in effect, only by hiring nonprofessionals to circumvent the traditional teaching division of labor. These study findings clearly imply that the conventional mode of school organization that most needs redesign in order that money may "make a difference," is the system for delivering instruction to children or, more specifically, the traditional work role of teachers.

The question should be raised whether the study observed teacher and paraprofessional employment situations and work results that are unique to the school setting in which the research was performed. The question cannot be answered definitely, and the answer lies with observations that would have to be made in other school settings. However, many observations suggest that most aspects of the employment situation in Portland, and staff responses to it, were not unique. In other school districts where we have knowledge about the manner in which teachers and paraprofessionals are employed, the pattern of utilization is much like the pattern in Portland. That is, paraprofessionals are often assigned to more than one teacher, teacher roles are not often redesigned to encourage specialization, and their aides tend to work primarily with small groups of children and not in classwide instruction when they teach. These employment patterns are probably a more or less universal function of the fact that schools do not have the resources to assign one aide to each teacher and paraprofessionals do not usually have training or experience to take command of entire class learning situations.

Because of these facts, our tendency is to believe that the study findings have more than general implications for other situations. Of course, situations in other school districts would not have to closely match the Portland scheme of things for the findings of this study to be relevant. Many school districts are experimenting with what is termed "diversified staffing" systems where the single classroom teacher role is abolished and team instruction of various kinds is used. The results of this study may be very useful for decisionmakers in those districts where attempts are being made to define new criteria for staff work arrangements.

Before this discussion of work study results is concluded, the outcome of some exploratory tests of relationships between staff characteristics and their work performance should be mentioned. Because the work observation data is unique information, the opportunity was taken to perform correlation analyses of relationships between such staff characteristics as age, education, experience, and their measured daily work patterns. These analyses had a purpose beyond pursuit of general interests. For cost effectiveness analysis purposes, it was useful to establish if the personal characteristics of the teacher and paraprofessional were associated with the kind and levels of work output measured in the study. If significant relationships were established, recommendations could be developed for assignment policies that might lead to more efficient utilization of staff.

However, correlation models with instruction and other work category times as independent variables and personal variables as dependent variables consistently produced low and insignificant correlation results. Models for paraprofessionals employing the same kind of variables had the same results. It seems probable that the very substantial differences that were measured in individual staff member work times contributed to these outcomes. Individual average category times were often a large multiple of averages of others in the population, and the dispersion and variance features of population measurements were not favorable for probability measurements. The experience with these analyses suggests the work observation measurements developed for this study are entirely useful for reviewing group work performance, but they are not especially valuable for assessing performance on the basis of individual differences. Some details of the statistical tests are reported in Appendix B.

Teacher and Paraprofessional Employment Costs

The work study results showed that instructional work could be increased significantly when paraprofessionals were added to staff in schools. With dimensions of relevant work now identified, this chapter considers costs the school district incurred when the work system was changed. The discussion deals with cost considerations from two perspectives. One perspective is concerned with cost and efficiency questions "in the small" at the level of the school operating systems. The relevant questions at this level pertain to identification of costs of hiring paraprofessionals and to the costs of producing units of instruction with alternative staff teaching assignments.

In the context of the overall cost effectiveness analysis, the key cost questions are whether the costs of the new work arrangements were in any way commensurable with educational benefits produced by those arrangements. This larger question is considered in later chapters after measures of benefits are reviewed. However, here preparations are made to consider that question by identifying the annual costs of the compensatory education program in Portland and the costs of teacher-paraprofessional teaming as part of that program. The first discussion in this chapter identifies costs of adding paraprofessionals to school staff. Later discussions compare costs of instruction for teacher-paraprofessional teams with conventional teacher costs and review annual labor costs of the school district.

Indirect Costs of Teacher and Paraprofessional Employment

The major new costs the Portland district experienced when the new instructional system was devised were salary costs of the paraprofessionals. These costs were readily identifiable in district records. However, indirect costs of bringing paraprofessionals into employment were not direct matters of record. Consequently, a major effort was made to survey these costs by interviews and study of district transactions. As was noted in Chapter 2, the evidence developed about indirect costs indicated that these costs were negligible. Recruiting costs were minimal because paraprofessionals were hired in circumstances where the supply of job applicants had always exceeded openings by very substantial margins. The district never found it necessary to incur costs of external recruiting search, and the costs of filling a vacancy were only a few dollars. Training costs were minimized because nonprofessionals were trained on the job. Additional facilities and materials costs attributable to paraprofessional employment were negligible.

All these findings indicated that direct salary costs of paraprofessionals were the only costs of the new work division that required consideration. The only significant fringe benefit costs incurred by the district were costs of federal social security taxes, the only financial benefit for nonprofessionals provided by the district. In the wage models elaborated below, the social security costs are not included in hourly wage averages used in the models. Readers should notice, therefore, that the labor cost figures are understated by relevant F.I.C.A. percentages.

None of the survey and interview information established that indirect costs of teacher employment were increased because of their work with paraprofessionals. Undoubtedly, there were minor increases in training and work opportunity costs, but these were too trivial to be enumerable. Moreover, costs of teacher recruitment and fringe benefits had dimensions that were at considerable disadvantage from the relatively trivial costs that were identified for paraprofessionals. A survey of recruiting costs determined that in the late 1960s these costs were approximately $100. per teacher hired for the Portland district. Moreover, teacher fringe benefit costs, principally for medical insurance, F.I.C.A., and retirement, were nearly 10 percent of the average annual salary costs.

The magnitudes of the annual salary differentials between teachers and paraprofessionals also demonstrate why employment of nonprofessionals can be financially attractive to school managers. The mean yearly salaries of all teachers who were included in the work study in the first research year was $7,818. The mean annual salary of paraprofessionals the same year was $4,149. Furthermore, paraprofessionals worked more hours daily although both groups worked on a 190 day annual contract basis. Teachers were scheduled to work a six and one-half hour day while paraprofessionals worked eight hours daily.

If school managers are satisfied that the quality of paraprofessional labor is not substantially inferior to the quality of teacher work inputs, then they would have every financial reason to employ and substitute some nonprofessional labor for that of teachers. To regard paraprofessional labor as a substitute for teacher labor appears appropriate. Should paraprofessional employment in the schools be prohibited by statutory means or by negotiated rules of employment, school managers would be required to employ professional teachers at much greater labor cost to perform substantially the same work that paraprofessionals perform. All the cost information developed in this study, including both direct and indirect labor cost observations, confirm substantial cost advantages for paraprofessional employment. Information in the remaining sections of this chapter provide a more detailed review of this comparative advantage.

Before instructional costs are analyzed in detail some limitations of the discussions in this chapter should be noted. It is most desirable, of course, that a cost-effectiveness analysis probe marginal cost relationships if the analysis can be performed with suitable data and without assumptions that strain credibility in order to build models. For the nonspecialist, and putting it briefly, marginal cost analysis is concerned with determining the incremental and extra costs that an organization incurs when it produces one extra or additional unit of output in the cheapest manner possible. The discussion in this chapter does not examine marginal cost relationships because district data were not available in forms that permitted meaningful analysis of this kind.

Because of these data limitations, the discussion in this chapter is concerned with average cost relationships. In the next chapter, however, important questions about labor costs and output are examined, and the analysis there concerns marginalist relationships using methods of linear programming. A linear programming model is elaborated that explores possibilities of an optimal work assignment mix for teacher and nonprofessional labor, a mix that maximizes total instructional work output within a cost minimization framework. In the less complex analyses that follow presently, however, the concern is with parameters of average hourly labor costs for staff.

Hourly Costs of Teacher and Nonprofessional Instruction

When aides are assigned to teachers, two salaries must be paid to obtain the total instruction and other work that the two staff members jointly produce. What are the labor costs of that jointly produced work, and how do combined teacher and paraprofessional costs of instruction compare to the costs for teachers working alone? These are key questions for purposes of determining the comparative efficiency of the alternative methods of organizing school work.

The discussion that follows focuses on comparative costs of producing hours of instructional time in the teacher with paraprofessional and the single teacher situations. The method used assumes that instructional time is the central productive output of teachers during the teaching day when children are at school. The essential method used for comparing costs of teacher labor was as follows.

First, for teachers working alone, the mean percentage of time those teachers spent in instructional activity for class hours of the day was computed from work study data. Teachers without nonprofessionals spent an average 31.13 percent of class hours in instructional activities. This figure differs slightly from the total daily percent of instruction reported in the work study because the 31.13 figure was calculated for the day after an allowance for free periods was made.

The hourly labor cost of instructional time was then calculated as follows: The 31.13 percentage figure was divided into the average hourly costs of teacher employment where average hourly costs were computed for a six-and one-half-hour day and also for an eight-hour day. The six-and one-half-hour day basis and the eight-hour day basis were both used for converting salaries to hourly rates for the following reasons.

Six and one-half hours were the total daily hours teachers were required to be at schools. However, eight hours per day, from the teachers' point of view, was more like the total labor hours expended by teachers when all preparations for class and other school activities were accounted for. For our illustrative purposes, either figure could be used. Use of the two daily hour figures is not undesirable because they provide comparative labor costs results for two different daily time assumptions.

Average hourly pay of teachers was $6.34 on the basis of a six-and one-half-hour day. The average hourly pay was $5.15 figured on the basis of an eight-hour day. The hourly wage figures were derived by determining the number of days worked per school year, dividing days worked into mean annual salary figures, and dividing the resulting mean daily salary figure by the hours worked per day figures, six and one-half and eight hours per day.

When the two hourly pay rate figures were obtained, both hourly rates were used, separately, to calculate the cost of producing an hour of instructional time. The method of calculation assumes, for illustrative purposes, that instruction time is the only valuable labor output that is produced in the class day. The method finds the number of hours that would have to be worked at $6.34 per hour (or at $5.15 per hour) in order to obtain one hour of instruction time. The calculations, for example, are:

$$\text{Hourly cost of instruction: } \frac{\$6.34}{31.13} = .2037 \times 100 = \$20.37$$

The result of the calculation can be read to mean that if 31.13 percent of each work hour is expended in instructional activities, then to obtain 1 hour of that activity, 3.21 labor hours each costing $6.34 will have to be expended at a total cost of $20.37.

The same method of calculation was used to find the hourly cost of producing teacher hours of instructional time that were devoted only to individual-small group instruction. This calculation was made because educators and administrators place special value on instruction that has intensive and tutorial dimensions for disadvantaged children. The hourly cost of individual-small group instruction for teachers without aides is $36.29.

Hourly costs of instructional activity by paraprofessionals and by teachers teamed with paraprofessionals were computed by a slightly different method that, nevertheless, provides comparable results. For these personnel, it was desirable to find hourly costs of instruction during periods when they worked together. The focus of concern was to find the instruction per hour that teacher-paraprofessional teams jointly produced, as well as the labor costs of the joint production. These figures would then be compared with the results for teachers working conventionally.

For this reason, the observation data from the work study were reviewed and the average hourly proportion of time that was spent in instructional activity by teachers and nonprofessionals, when they were teamed, was computed. Teachers spent an average 41.8 percent of their time in instructional activity. The paraprofessionals expended an average 51.6 percent of the time in instructional activity. Their individual-small group instructional time was 51.3 percent.

The hourly cost figure for instructional hours produced by teachers and paraprofessionals when they were teamed was computed in the following manner. First, costs for an hour of instruction and for individual-small group instruction were determined separately for teachers and for paraprofessionals. For example:

Hourly cost of instruction for teamed teacher: $\dfrac{\$6.34}{41.8} = 1516 \times 100 = \$15.16$

The hourly cost for paraprofessionals, assuming a $2.73 hourly rate on an eight-hour day basis, and with 51.6 percent of time expended in instruction is $5.29. Figured the same way, the hourly cost for individual-small group instruction for teachers is $18.71 and the hourly cost of the same kind of instruction for paraprofessionals is $5.32. For identification purposes, classwide instruction will be designated "IN" and individual-small group instruction will be designated "IN_2."

Having derived the separate costs of hours of instruction for teachers and for paraprofessionals, the next step is to combine their separate costs by a method that gives the cost for an hour of instruction that is produced jointly. Assuming, meanwhile, that one time unit of paraprofessional instruction is equal in quality to one time unit of teacher instruction, the method is:

Cost per hour of team jointly produced IN $= \dfrac{\$15.16 + \$5.29}{2} = \$10.22$

Cost per hour of team jointly produced $IN_2 = \dfrac{\$18.71 + \$5.32}{2} = \$12.01$

And the same costs per team hour when teacher wages are assumed to be $5.15 per hour are:

Cost per hour of team jointly produced IN = $8.80

Cost per hour of team jointly produced IN_2 = $10.26

The hourly costs results for IN and IN_2 hours for the teacher and paraprofessional teams show a substantial cost advantage over the teacher without paraprofessional hourly cost of $20.27 for IN and $36.29 for IN_2 hours.

One more aspect of methods of calculation needs to be considered before results are summarized. The above calculations do not account for possible differences in the quality of teacher and paraprofessional instruction. All the calculations added time units of instruction for teachers and their aides without quality weights for differences in the quality of work.

Questions about the relative quality of teacher and paraprofessional instruction were often discussed with personnel in the school district. Few persons thought there was a large disparity in quality of instruction by any standard. But few believed the average paraprofessional was as competent as the average teacher. As is usual in qualitative comparisons, it proved difficult to obtain precise comparisons.

For this reason, a quality weighting device was devised for cost comparisons. Refer to Table 6-1. The first table column is headed "Quality Weight For Paraprofessional IN Hour." If one is inclined to believe, for whatever reasons, that one hour of paraprofessional instruction would be worth only 90, or 80, or a lesser percentage of one hour of teacher instruction, then the hourly cost figure in the next column under the heading "Joint Hourly Cost of IN For Teacher-Paraprofessional Team" indicates the team cost of instruction at the percentage weighting selected. Thus if an observer believes that a paraprofessional's instruction is of equal quality, or worth 100 percent of teacher instruction, the hourly cost is $10.22 for an hour of instruction produced by the teacher and paraprofessional team.

The hourly cost figures for the percentage weights were derived in the following way. If it is assumed that paraprofessional instruction is only 50 percent as valuable as teacher instruction, then the weighting system increases the total teacher and paraprofessional hourly instructional cost by 50 percent of the paraprofessional's hourly cost of instruction. This is not an entirely arbitrary scheme. If a paraprofessional's value productivity is assumed to decline 50 percent per unit of time worked, the unit cost of labor could increase by the same amount.

The weighting system is arbitrary only in the limited sense that readers are permitted to make their own judgments concerning appropriate quality weights for instruction. The other percentage weights were computed in the same manner with appropriate cost weightings for 60 percent, 70 percent, etc. The hourly cost figures in the table for teachers without paraprofessionals, of course, require no such weighting scheme.

Two tables are presented with Table 6-1 data calculated on the basis of average teacher hourly pay costs of $6.34 based on a six and one-half hour day. Table 6-2 differs from Table 6-1 only because data in Table 6-2 are computed with average teacher hourly pay of $5.15 based on an 8 hour day. Two tables were made with the two teacher rates to demonstrate how costs would differ

Table 6-1

Average Hourly Costs of Instructional Time for Teacher-Paraprofessional Team and Teachers without Paraprofessionals

Quality Weight for Paraprofessional IN Hour	Joint Hourly Cost of IN for Teacher-Paraprofessional Team (Teacher Rate $6.34/Hour)	Hourly Cost of IN for Teacher without Paraprofessionals
Paraprofessional hour = 100% teacher hour	$10.22	$20.37
Paraprofessional hour = 90% teacher hour	10.52	20.37
Paraprofessional hour = 80% teacher hour	10.88	20.37
Paraprofessional hour = 70% teacher hour	11.36	20.37
Paraprofessional hour = 60% teacher hour	11.99	20.37
Paraprofessional hour = 50% teacher hour	12.86	20.37

Quality Weight for Paraprofessional IN_2 Hour	Joint Hourly Cost of IN_2 for Teacher-Paraprofessional Team (Teacher Rate $6.34/Hour)	Hourly Cost of IN_2 for Teacher without Paraprofessional
Paraprofessional hour = 100% teacher hour	$12.01	$36.29
Paraprofessional hour = 90% teacher hour	12.31	36.29
Paraprofessional hour = 80% teacher hour	12.69	36.29
Paraprofessional hour = 70% teacher hour	13.15	36.29
Paraprofessional hour = 60% teacher hour	13.79	36.29
Paraprofessional hour = 50% teacher hour	14.67	36.29

Table 6-2
Average Hourly Costs of Invidual-Small Group Instruction Time for Teacher-Paraprofessional Team and Teachers without Paraprofessionals

Quality Weight for Paraprofessional IN Hour	Joint Hourly Cost of IN for Teacher-Paraprofessional Team (Teacher Rate $5.15/Hour)	Hourly Cost of IN for Teacher without Paraprofessional
Paraprofessional Hour = 100% teacher hour	$8.80	$16.54
Paraprofessional Hour = 90% teacher hour	9.09	16.54
Paraprofessional Hour = 80% teacher hour	9.46	16.54
Paraprofessional Hour = 70% teacher hour	9.93	16.54
Paraprofessional Hour = 60% teacher hour	10.56	16.54
Paraprofessional Hour = 50% teacher hour	11.44	16.54

Quality Weight for Paraprofessional IN_2 Hour	Joint Hourly Cost of IN_2 for Teacher-Paraprofessional Team (Teacher Rate $5.15/Hour)	Hourly Cost of IN_2 for Teacher without Paraprofessional
Paraprofessional hour = 100% teacher hour	$10.26	$29.43
Paraprofessional hour = 90% teacher hour	10.55	29.43
Paraprofessional hour = 80% teacher hour	10.92	29.43
Paraprofessional hour = 70% teacher hour	11.40	29.43
Paraprofessional hour = 60% teacher hour	12.03	29.43
Paraprofessional hour = 50% teacher hour	12.93	29.43

under two assumptions about the length of the paid work day. The average paraprofessional hourly rate is $2.73 in both tables, based on an eight-hour work day.

The table results provide significant comparisons. First, in both Table 6-1 and Table 6-2, the hourly costs of instruction are considerably lower for the teacher-paraprofessional team in comparison to the single teacher. This is true for both IN and IN_2.

In Table 6-1, with teacher pay rate $6.34 hourly, the teacher-paraprofessional hourly costs range from $12.86 to $10.22 at given quality weights. And for an hour of IN_2, the costs are from $14.67 to $12.01. The comparative cost per hour for a single teacher is $20.37 for IN and $36.29 for IN_2. Large cost differences are also reported in Table 6-2 where the figures differ only because they were calculated assuming a $5.15 hourly pay rate for teachers.

An interesting result is that the tables show a considerable cost advantage for the teacher-paraprofessional team even when the quality of paraprofessional instruction is negatively weighted most heavily. In Table 6-1, the cost figure for teacher-paraprofessional IN increases only from $10.22 to $12.86 when the negative quality weight is shifted from 100 percent to 50 percent. But even the $12.86 cost at 50 percent quality weight is much below the single teacher hourly IN cost figure of $20.36. The same general result holds for IN_2 costs at weight 50 percent where the comparative figures are $14.67 vs. $36.29.

There is more than a hint here that even if paraprofessional quality of instruction varies considerably the comparative value of team instruction will remain quite advantageous. The reasons for this comparative cost result are linked to benefits obtained by the inclusion of paraprofessionals in the division of labor. The first and most obvious reason is that hourly costs of employing paraprofessionals were so much less expensive than teacher hourly costs. Paraprofessional hourly costs were $2.73 on an eight-hour day basis. Teacher hourly costs were $5.15 on the same eight-hour basis.

The second reason is that paraprofessionals produced more IN per hour than teachers with or without paraprofessionals. Teachers working with paraprofessionals produced slightly more IN in the class hours that their assistants worked directly with them in class. But obviously it was the paraprofessional production of 51 percent IN per hour worked with teachers that made almost all the difference. For educational programs with remedial objectives, and ones that prized more tutorial instructional emphases, the considerably lower costs of IN, and especially IN_2, would be particularly valuable cost effectiveness outcomes.

Limitations of the Cost Analysis

The hourly instructional cost analysis is a special purpose analysis. The objective was to demonstrate relative costs per hour of instruction for teacher-paraprofessional teams in comparison to conventional single teacher arrangements. For illustrative purposes, the analysis assumed that hours of instructional input are the principal valuable products of teacher and paraprofessional labor. This is not an unreasonable assumption, but the analysis was not meant to indicate that teachers and paraprofessionals might not produce other valuable services in their work in schools.

And, of course, the school district had to pay the total of teachers' and paraprofessionals' annual salaries to obtain instructional and other services the teams produced. The analysis has shown that hourly costs of instruction were cheaper for the teams. But if one relaxes the assumption that instruction is the sole valuable service produced, the implications of the foregoing illustrative analysis are altered.

Apart from any illustrative analyses, the data of this study indicate more generally that the district was able to purchase more than 100 percent additional instruction, in comparison to instruction produced by single teachers, when paraprofessionals were teamed with teachers. And this additional instruction was obtained from nonprofessionals whose labor costs were approximately 50 percent of teacher labor costs.

The analyses and observations in this section are special purpose analyses that examine detailed production processes. They are not the only cost analyses of the compensatory program, for others are reported in the next section. Here the concern has been to focus on special details of micro labor cost parameters. The following chapter continues this focus where it employs a linear programming model to identify teacher and paraprofessional work assignment patterns that have special cost and output advantages. The remainder of this chapter is concerned with the broader dimension of costs and identifies annual costs the district experienced for the compensatory program and for team instruction as a part of the program.

Preliminaries to a Review of
Annual Program Costs

The examination of hourly instructional costs for teachers and nonprofessionals was concerned with cost and work output relationships for instruction alone. The discussion in this section reviews the more comprehensive costs of the compensatory program on an annual basis for the years 1964-65 to 1965-70. For this analysis, district cost records for all the years were examined and program costs per child, or more precisely, per average daily membership, were computed.[a] The

[a]Average Daily Membership (ADM) represents the average daily number of children who were enrolled in the schools during the year. Average daily attendance figures would be more desirable statistics for cost computations because they would more accurately reflect the literal number of children served, but attendance figures were not available to identify student participation for all schools for all the years. Use of ADM produces slightly reduced average costs per child. The ratio of ADM to average daily attendance for the district ranged between 1.11 and 1.07 for the years 1965-66 to 1969-70.

districtwide costs for average daily membership in nonprogram elementary schools were also computed for the same years. The result is that average annual ADM costs for the program schools and for the rest of the district can be compared to determine what additional or incremental resources were expended for the program.

The particular components of average costs that are of greatest interest for this study are average costs per ADM for instruction in conventional teaching arrangements, as compared to ADM instructional costs for compensatory program schools. Subsequently, when measures of average program benefits are obtained, we shall want to relate the additional average costs of teacher-nonprofessional team instruction to average program benefit levels for purposes of drawing cost-effectiveness conclusions.

The results of the cost analyses that follow will not permit us to judge if program expenditures were necessarily expended efficiently. Nor will they permit identification of annual costs for the new teacher-paraprofessional team instruction that can be specifically correlated with student achievement gains or other benefits that may have been produced by that instruction. Ideally, we should like to derive such coefficients, but data could not be obtained from district sources that permitted calculation of coefficients or marginal costs and benefits.

In order to derive meaningful coefficients of association between program costs, inputs, and benefits, it would be necessary to obtain measurements of instructional inputs for large samples of teachers and paraprofessionals and to measure their work over long time periods coincident with the period for which achievement gains were being measured. Information about program costs and annual test scores was available in the district. However, even the comprehensive work study could not provide data about instructional inputs that was sufficiently comprehensive for correlation analysis.

However, even with this limitation, the cost analyses presented in this chapter may bring us tolerably close to firm conclusions about the cost effectiveness of the teacher-paraprofessional division of work. The earlier analysis in this chapter showed that instruction was produced at much more effective labor cost ratios when paraprofessionals were employed. If this present analysis indicates that the annual costs per student of employing paraprofessionals was very substantially below teacher employment costs, this additional information will reinforce cost effectiveness conclusions favorable to their employment. Furthermore, the method of approach subsequently will be to compare annual ADM labor cost averages of teachers and paraprofessionals with average benefit gains the compensatory program achieved. Because it is known from the work study data that paraprofessionals produced more average instruction than did teachers daily, this comparison should also have meaningful cost effectiveness implications.

Annual Costs of the Compensatory Program

In order to identify the annual average costs of employing teachers and paraprofessionals in Portland, it was necessary to establish the comprehensive annual costs of operating Portland elementary schools and derive labor cost averages from this more general information. Annual current costs for the operation of each elementary school in the Portland district for the years 1965-70 could be identified in district records. Calculations were then made to identify the average annual current costs of operating those district schools that participated in the compensatory program. The statistic of main interest is the figure for annual current costs because these costs, so defined, are costs of school operations that vary according to the number of students taught in a given year, or for present purposes, that vary according to ADM. Expenditures in the following categories are included in the annual current cost data:

1. Costs of instruction
2. Costs of instructional materials
3. Costs of attendance, health, and related services
4. Costs of school administrative services
5. Costs of operation of school plant
6. Costs of maintenance of school plant

The total of these costs for schools does not include noncurrent and long-term capital expenditures which have a more remote and less readily definable relationship to per-pupil services.

For the school years 1964-65 to 1969-70, the resources for all district elementary schools had the following sources. All elementary schools, including those in the compensatory program, were principally supported by funds from local sources. However, additional funds for the program beyond local sources were provided by federal government Title I funds and special state funds that were available for some of the years.

In the discussion, annual average current operating costs per ADM for all district schools and for schools in the compensatory program are identified for the years 1964-65 to 1969-70. The costs identified include local, state, and federal cost contributions for any of the years when those sources made contributions. In addition to annual current operating costs, annual instructional costs as a component of operating costs are identified.

Costs for the year 1964-65 will be considered first. This is a key comparison year because it was the last year before the program was initiated and special funds were expended in program schools. Table 6-3 reports average annual costs of current operations per ADM for the district. In 1964-65 these annual ADM costs were $470 for all the elementary schools in the district.

In the first compensatory program year 1965-66, district average current

Table 6-3
Average Annual Costs of Current Operations per ADM, Program and Nonprogram Schools, 1964-65 to 1969-70

Years	1964-65	1965-66	1966-67	1967-68	1968-69	1969-70
District mean annual cost of current operations per ADM, all elementary schools	$470	$507	$540	$545	$600	$650
Federal contribution to annual cost of per ADM current operations, program schools		259	229	187	175	157
State contribution to annual cost of per ADM current operations, program schools				167	262	278
Total annual per ADM cost of current operations, program schools only	$470	$766	$769	$899	$1037	$1085
Difference in mean annual cost of per ADM current operations, program and all other elementary schools	$000	$259	$229	$354	$437	$435

costs per ADM for all elementary schools were $507. The first annual federal contribution to program schools was $259 per ADM. The total local and federal contribution to program schools was $766 per ADM.

In 1966-67 local expenditures for all schools increased to $540 per ADM for average current operations costs. The federal cost contribution to the program declined slightly with the result that average total current expenditures per ADM were $769, or at almost the same level as for 1965-66.

From 1967-68 through 1969-70, local average total current cost expenditures for all schools increased approximately $50 per year. The result was that by 1969-70 average current operations costs per ADM were $650, an amount that exceeded the figure for the last preprogram year 1964-65 by $180.

In addition, from 1967-68 on, other special state funds contributed to the program. These contributions added $167 per ADM for average total current costs in 1967-68, $262 per ADM in 1968-69, and $278 per ADM in 1969-70. These special state funds were sufficient to offset a decline in federal funding that occurred from 1967-68 through 1969-70.

Therefore, from 1964-65 to 1969-70 average total current costs per ADM in program schools increased from $470 to $1085. During those years, the district increased its contribution by the additional $180 per ADM that was expended for all district schools. The district expended another $50 additional by 1969-70 for program schools only, an amount that is not shown separately in the table because it was expended with state matching funds in the state special program contributions. Federal cost contributions declined from 1966-67 on, but this decline was more than made up for by state cost contributions beginning in 1967-68 that increased through 1969-70.

A key comparison in Table 6-3 is the comparison between the 1969-70 district figure for average current operating costs per ADM, which is $650, and the 1969-70 figure of $1085 for a total annual per ADM cost of current operations in program schools. When the former $650 figure is subtracted from the $1085, the resulting $435 is the amount of extraordinary or additional costs that were expended per ADM annually by 1969-70 for the compensatory program. The $435 figure per ADM is almost as large as the district's average ADM cost of current operations in all elementary schools in the year 1964-65, the year before the program was initiated. The similar additional cost figures for each of the years from 1965-66 were $259 for 1965-66, $229 for 1966-67, $354 for 1967-68, and $437 for 1968-69.

Table 6-4 provides the same kind of breakdown of costs as Table 6-3, but in this instance the table reports average annual cost of instruction per ADM. Instructional costs, of course, are a component of average annual current operating costs and represent largely costs of salaries and benefits for teaching staff. As that table shows, the district's average annual costs of instruction per ADM for all elementary schools increased from $363 in 1964-65 to $520 in 1969-70. For the program schools, however, the cost of instruction per ADM

Table 6-4
Average Annual Costs of Instruction per ADM, Program and Nonprogram Schools, 1964-65 to 1969-70

Years	1964-65	1965-66	1966-67	1967-68	1968-69	1969-70
District mean annual cost of instruction per ADM, all elementary schools	$363	$390	$416	$435	$470	$520
Federal contribution to annual cost of per ADM instruction, program schools		182	204	159	153	114
State contribution to annual cost of per ADM instruction, program schools				95	186	206
Total annual per ADM cost of instruction, program schools only	$363	$572	$620	$689	$809	$840
Difference in mean annual cost of instruction, per ADM, program and all other elementary schools	$000	$182	$204	$254	$339	$320

increased in the same period from $363 to $840, and the greatest part of this increase was funded by a combination of state and federal contributions. The additional or "extra" average cost per ADM for instruction increased to $320 during the five-year period, as the fifth row in the table indicates. This $320 figure is the difference between the all district cost of $520 for 1969-70 and the $840 per ADM cost total for instruction in program schools in 1969-70.

The point bears repeating that these average cost figures cannot be reviewed for purposes of appraising the strict efficiency of the compensatory program. Judgments about efficiency in a formal sense could be made only by comparing average or marginal costs of the program with comprehensive measures of average or marginal benefits. And valid judgments about cost and benefit dimensions could be made only if it were known that a program and its components were efficient in their detailed operating arrangements. In the absence of data suitable for marginal cost analysis, however, the data here showing average ADM costs are most useful for identifying extraordinary program labor costs. And the data can be used to isolate that proportion of annual program costs that were attributable to the introduction of paraprofessionals and the new costs of modifying the division of labor.

Costs of Paraprofessional Employment as a Proportion of Program Costs

The comments made above about efficiency apply equally well to the following review of program labor costs for paraprofessional employment. The discussion will indicate that annual costs of paraprofessional employment, the principal new costs associated with the new division, were a very small proportion of annual total costs of program instruction. Because it has been established that paraprofessionals produced significantly more instruction per day than more expensive teachers, the conclusion will be that they contributed to new instruction produced in the program to a degree that was very effective, given their relative costs and their numbers as a proportion of all additional staff that was added to program schools.

Table 6-4 reported that the total average instructional costs per ADM for the years 1965-66 to 1969-70 were in a range from $572 to $840. And the additional program instructional costs per ADM that were expended beyond all-district average costs ranged from $182 to $320 during the five years. For those years, the average annual per ADM costs of paraprofessional labor in the program schools were $30 for 1965-66 and between $67 and $78 for the years from 1967-68 to.1969-70. These figures are not shown separately in Table 6-4. It is apparent that average annual costs of paraprofessional employment were a very small proportion of total additional costs of program instruction.

Table 6-5 identifies the number of classroom and special teachers and

Table 6-5
Numbers of Teachers and Paraprofessionals Employed in Compensatory Program Schools, 1964-1969

Year	Number of Teachers	Number of Paraprofessionals
1964	237	—
1965	274	42
1966	276	90
1967	(no data available)	
1968	293	90
1969	297	87

paraprofessional aides that were employed in the program schools during all the years, except 1967-68. The number of teachers that were added after 1964-65 to improve instruction was between thirty-seven and sixty during the program years. These additional teachers are the major source of increased average ADM instructional costs that ranged from $182 to $320 in the years of the program.

During the same years, with the exception of 1965-66, nearly ninety paraprofessionals were employed at average annual costs per ADM that ranged from $67 to $78. Therefore, the number of paraprofessionals introduced to the division of labor when the program commenced was significantly more than the number of teachers, but the proportion of all additional instructional costs of the program that was attributable to paraprofessionals was markedly less than the proportion attributable to new teachers. Furthermore, it is known from the work study that paraprofessionals produced more instruction than teachers, and very much more individual and small-group remedial instruction.

Because significantly more paraprofessionals were employed than teachers at much lower average ADM and hourly employment costs and because of their relative work production, it is reasonable to conclude they made contributions within the division of school labor that were very effective in proportion to their relative costs of employment. Additional conclusions about these contributions may be deferred until more is reported about the benefits that the program realized.

7 A Quantitative Model of a Teaching Division of Labor

The observations from the work study revealed previously unknown facts about the nature of teacher and paraprofessional work. From the beginning of the research, the work study was conceived as an effort with multiple research purposes. One of these was to provide work observation data that could be used in efforts to model the new school division of labor mathematically. In this chapter, a quantitative model is identified that utilizes the work study data. Elaboration of the model makes it possible to press beyond the immediate work study observations which could describe only existing relationships. By manipulating the work observations quantitatively, the model extends the range of insights work study data offers.

Many readers will not be familiar with methods of operations research and, in particular, techniques of linear programming, the method for modeling used in this study. For this reason, choices about the level of complexity to be pursued in the analysis were presented to us. One opportunity was to make an extensive analysis of the program in the Portland district that could focus on many real problems and constraints decisionmakers faced in that city. The chief limitation of a complex analysis of this kind would be that many details of analysis and solution would be particular to the situation in that city. Our choice, therefore, was to elaborate a less complicated analysis that accounted for the more important problems school decisionmakers would encounter in making decisions about costs and employment in a new division of labor. The resulting model is more comprehensible to persons without special quantitative training, and the model results are generalizable to a greater variety of settings. For the benefit of readers who are not familiar with linear programming methods, a few words about these methods will be useful.

Decisionmakers in institutions continually deal with the problem of deciding what services or products shall be produced, what methods should be used to produce them, and what resources should be committed in relevant production processes. Decisions of this sort lie at the heart of management and administration, whether one is concerned with producing physical goods, or the concern is with provision of services to persons, as in education. In private firms or public institutions like schools, administrators make choices for transforming resources from one form to another more valuable form, and they have alternatives to consider for the most effective way to make these changes.

There are usually many different ways resources can be combined to obtain services or goods in desired amounts and quality. The problem of choosing the correct inputs of resources, the best production processes, and the most desirable product or service outputs is often formidable. Consider the complexities involved in a school decision to employ teachers and nonprofessionals in a new division of labor. Immediately complex problems of choice arise, including choices for the number of staff to employ at what budget level, the method of assigning staff to work, choice of tasks to include in the new division of labor, and many other interrelated matters. This complex mix of work, production, and cost questions can be greatly clarified, if not entirely solved, by linear programming methods. This is a mathematical technique for establishing the most economic or desirable plan of action for production circumstances where the problem can be expressed in linear terms, several variables are under consideration, and many alternative problem approaches are feasible. Linear programming problems are concerned with the maximization or minimization of a linear objective function subject to linear constraints in the model equations. If a problem solution can be stated as the minimization or maximization of the sum of several variables that are linearly related and if variable combinations may be restricted to ranges of values established by a linear relationship, then linear programming methods can be used to find a solution to the problem.

With the information available from the work study that identifies daily work category times for teachers and nonprofessionals, and with labor cost information available also, it is possible to design linear programming models to probe a number of instruction production questions. In the context of this study and its purposes, a most worthwhile question concerns the appropriate number and mix of teacher and paraprofessionals to hire to maximize total instruction for children with a given budget for employment of staff. The average hourly costs of teacher and paraprofessional labor are known and can be expressed in linear terms. The work study also established the average amounts of instruction, routine, and other work tasks that staff produced per hour worked. These average work times and labor costs as well as their ratio to each other per hour are all susceptible to expression in linear terms as is required for the linear programming method.

The linear programming model discussed in this chapter determines an optimal mix of teacher and paraprofessional assignments in the instructional division of labor. The purpose for designing the model is to establish a method that will allow us to make a comparative cost analysis and a staffing assignment plan when the influence of different labor costs and amounts of teacher and nonprofessional productive work are entered into equations in the model.

The model treats total teaching time of teachers and nonprofessionals as the variable in the division of labor that is to be maximized in model solution results. Instructional time is the variable to be maximized under the assumption that instruction is the central productive and valuable output of the division of labor for education at this level. In addition, the rationale for introducing nonprofessionals into the division is to increase total instruction by allowing teachers to instruct more while their aides also teach and assume teachers' nonprofessional work.

The model considers a hypothetical school situation and identifies the maximum instructional time that can be produced by different assignments of teachers and nonprofessionals when different values of their employment costs and amounts of their instructional and other task times are considered. Some special features of the model are that it finds the optimal distribution of teaching time between teachers and nonprofessionals, given a school labor budget, the scheduled number of class hours that must be met, ratios of routine and other work times to teaching time, and other model characteristics specified below.

A central objective in model design was to produce a model useful for illustrative purposes that can be generalized to different settings. The model does not include a number of variables that might have been entered if the model were to be implemented in Portland or another particular school district. The model includes essential characteristics of the division of labor in the analysis. Because it considers essentials, the results suggested by the model solution may be more readily applicable in diverse settings because only one or a small number of variables would have to be added or changed to fit the facts of other situations.

The solution obtained by the model is for a hypothetical school situation where it is assumed:

1. there are 20 elementary classrooms;
2. twenty teachers are employed in the 20 classrooms;
3. five paraprofessionals are employed in the school;
4. each paraprofessional is assigned to work with 4 teachers;
5. each teacher works 5 class hours a day;
6. each paraprofessional works 5 class hours a day;
7. total daily class hours for all teachers are 5 X 20 = 100;
8. total daily class hours for all paraprofessionals are 5 X 5 = 25; and
9. total labor costs daily for all staff are $919.25 where:
   20 teachers are each paid $8.08 hourly for 5 hours and
   5 paraprofessionals are each paid $4.29 hourly for 5 hours.

The assumptions above are all based on real Portland school data observations for costs, staffing ratios, and hours. However, the details of assumptions could be changed to suit other situations. For example, the numbers of staff could be altered as would fit circumstances in other districts. And the scheduled daily hours of classes and hours worked could be changed to represent weekly or monthly time periods. The utility of the general model, therefore, is that it may be used as a generalizable model for indicating how the division of work might be changed in plural settings, but the specific data used in the application of the model is derived from real facts of the Portland situation.

In operation, and as the model determines an optimal work task mix for N teachers and N nonprofessionals, it uses the average values of Instruction, Routine, and other work categories that were observed in the Portland work study. It was necessary, nevertheless, to alter these work category variables to a minor extent in order to fit requirements of the model. The rationale and method for making these changes in the data were as follows.

A requirement of the model was that it have the capability to substitute minute units of task times for teachers and paraprofessionals in order to arrive at a solution for optimal work patterns in the division of labor between staff. The work study had obtained observations for teacher and paraprofessional Instruction, Routine, and other task categories as separate and distinct work categories. No Instruction, for example, was also identified as Routine. That discrete categorical separation was appropriate because the objective of the work study was to divide daily work time into time expended in particular task categories.

However, the question might be raised: Is there some irreducible amount of routine task time teachers must perform to be able to teach? If teachers must perform some minimum amount of routine tasks while they teach, it would be a mistake to design a model that assumes teachers solely instruct in the alternative work arrangements the model considers. Such an assumption would deny that even a fully specialized teacher would have to perform some minimum routine tasks, such as entering class and dispersing materials before lessons could begin.

Because it was recognized that some routine, nonlearning, and other tasks might hypothetically be associated with production of instruction, the model could not assume units of "pure" IN could be substituted for other tasks in model calculations. In order to overcome this problem, the work study observations for subjects were reviewed, and wherever it was determined that subjects had performed routine or nonlearning tasks immediately before or after they performed instruction units, these routine and nonlearning task times were isolated from similar tasks not closely associated with instruction.

The task times that subjects had expended in these isolated routine and nonlearning tasks were then combined with instructional task times of subjects to create a new variable that will be termed NIN. The utility of NIN for the linear programming model is that the new variable permits assignment of NIN task times to teachers and paraprofessionals, and it makes appropriate distinction between total task times committed to instruction and work activity not related to instruction. We cannot be absolutely sure that all the routine and nonlearning activities we identified and included in NIN were necessary for the production of instruction. But if errors in identification and assignment of these tasks did occur, the result would not be very damaging to the analysis and model solution. Erroneous inclusion of some routine and nonlearning time not actually associated with IN would only produce a model solution with slightly more conservative instructional maximization parameters.

The review of work study data for the periods when staff were in classes indicated teachers spent an average 57.9 percent of their class hours in NIN activity. They spent 34.1 percent of their class hours in routine not required for instruction. They also expended 8.0 percent of hours in all other tasks not required for teaching: evaluation, administration, nonlearning, and others. In the calculations for the model, these other tasks are combined in one category designated Oth (other tasks).

In the model, NIN_t and NIN_a identify the new learning time variables for teachers and aides. NIN_t and NIN_a are the work time variables to be maximized in the linear programming solution. The model provides that hours of routine and "other" task times are to be minimized in order to recognize, as the work study indicated, that classes cannot function unless some minimum of routine and other tasks are performed.

Before the objective function and constraints associated with it are identified, it will be useful to state some definitions of terms. The definitions are:

NIN_t	=	the number of hours of teacher teaching time, including minimum related necessary tasks;
NIN_a	=	the number of hours of aide teaching time, including minimum related necessary tasks;
$ROUT_t$	=	the number of hours of teacher routine time not associated with instruction;
$ROUT_a$	=	the number of hours of paraprofessional routine time not associated with instruction;
OTH_t	=	the number of hours of "other" teacher task time not associated with instruction;
OTH_a	=	the number of hours of "other" paraprofessional task time not associated with instruction;
a_1, a_2	=	relative weights for NIN_t and NIN_a;
$c_1, c_2, c_3,$ c_4, c_5, c_6	=	cost coefficients for teacher and paraprofessional task times: NIN_t, NIN_a, etc.;
$d_1\, ROUT_t$	=	the proportion of routine task time done by teachers in the division;
$d_1\, OTH_t$	=	the proportion of other task time done by teachers in the division;
$d_2\, ROUT_a$	=	the proportion of routine task time done by paraprofessionals in the division;
$d_2\, OTH_a$	=	the proportion of "other" task time done by paraprofessionals in the division;
K	=	the minimum number of hours of NIN_t performed per day;
p_1	=	the proportion of Rout required per hour of NIN_t;
p_2	=	the proportion of Oth required per hour of NIN_t; and
X	=	the total daily budget for teachers and aides.

Explanation of some of these definitions is desirable. It will be useful also to specify briefly how the computation procedure deals with some of the variables.

In the hypothetical school situation for which calculations are made, teachers and paraprofessionals work a daily total of 125 class hours. What the model basically accomplishes is computation of the maximum number of $NIN_t + NIN_a$ hours that can be obtained in the school teaching day, given the proportions of NIN, Rout, and Oth that teachers and paraprofessionals perform to all daily time, and given their relative labor costs, the possibilities of reassigning tasks, and certain other restrictions in the model.

The NIN, Rout, and Oth variables for teachers and paraprofessionals serve to identify those work categories in hourly units, as the model computes and reallocates category times among teachers and paraprofessionals. The computation procedure always maintains the sum of the three categories, however they are subdivided, as the total of all daily class hours.

The variables a_1 and a_2 provide relative weights for NIN_t and NIN_a in hourly task proportion terms as the division is calculated.

The d_1 and d_2 variables and the p_1 and p_2 variables have their origins in the average daily task times the work study identified for teachers and paraprofessionals. For example, it was determined that teachers worked 34.1 percent of daily class time in Rout activities. This figure was then used to determine that the proportion of Rout required per hour of NIN_t was .587. The model uses this proportion and similarly derived proportions for p_2, d_1, and d_2 to divide the total 125 work hours among NIN, Rout, and Oth tasks for staff (even as other model specifications are considered simultaneously).

The cost coefficients weight for changing hourly labor costs of teachers and paraprofessionals as staff perform more or less of different work categories. The coefficients have their basis in mean hourly pay rates as computed for school staff.

K, the minimum hours of NIN_t performed per day, has a basis in work study data that indicated the proportion of NIN_t per day to all work hours was .579. This indicates that 20 teachers working a total 100 daily hours would produce 57.9 hours of NIN_t. The model uses the 57.9 figure as a minimum weight for computing NIN_t in proportion to other task categories as the model forces reallocation of task hours between teachers and paraprofessionals.

The total daily labor budget, X is \$915.25.

The objective function of the model is subject to restrictions included in order to constrain the maximizing solution by acknowledging different labor cost ratios for teacher and paraprofessional work units, the total labor budget limit, minimum teaching hours required, and other constraints. The objective function is:

$$\text{MAX } a_1 \, NIN_t + a_2 \, NIN_a - ROUT_t - ROUT_a - OTH_t - OTH_a$$
subject to these restrictions:

(1) c_1 NIN$_t$ + c_2 NIN$_a$ + c_3 ROUT$_t$ + c_4 ROUT$_a$ + c_5 OTH$_t$ + c_6 OTH$_a$ $\leqslant X$

(2) p_1 NIN$_t$ − ROUT$_t$ − ROUT$_a$ $\leqslant 0$

(3) p_2 NIN$_t$ − OTH$_t$ − OTH$_a$ $\leqslant 0$

(4) NIN$_t$ $\geqslant K$

(5) NIN$_t$ NIN$_a$ ROUT$_t$ ROUT$_a$ OTH$_t$ OTH$_a$ $\geqslant 0$

(6) d_1 ROUT$_t$ − d_2 ROUT$_a$ $\leqslant 0$

(7) d_1 OTH$_t$ − d_2 OTH$_a$ $\leqslant 0$

The reader who is unfamiliar with symbolic conventions should be assured the above statements are not complicated. Considered separately, they may be understood to mean the following:

The objective function is the function whose value is to be maximized, subject to the stated restrictions. The function in verbal terms states that the relative weights of the number of teacher and paraprofessional instruction hours per day are to be maximized, less the necessary hours of teacher and paraprofessional routine and "other" task time that are performed in the work day.

The solution for the objective function is clearly concerned with maximizing the NIN variables, and not the variables Rout and Oth. But the model acknowledges that minimum hours of Rout and Oth are necessary during the hours of the class day. The restrictions placed upon the objective function indicate the following constraints exist:

(1) states that the total costs of the number of hours of the different tasks performed may not exceed the labor budget.

(2) indicates the product of the proportion of routine tasks required per hour of NIN$_t$ and the number of hours of NIN$_t$ hours shall be equal or less than zero when the number of hours of staff routine hours worked are subtracted from that product. In the linear programming computations, inequalities become equalities in the optimal solution, and this statement permits estimation of p_1 which is ROUT$_t$ + ROUT$_a$ = .587 X NIN$_t$.

(3) states the same kind of restriction as in (2) above; in this case the inequality permits estimation of p_2 which is OTH$_t$ + OTH$_a$ = .138 X NIN$_t$.

(4) states that the number of hours of teacher Instructional time shall be equal to or greater than the minimum number of hours of NIN$_t$ performed per day. NIN$_t$ was 57.9 hours for all teachers in the hypothetical school, and this statement sets a minimum of NIN$_t$ for purposes of forcing an allocation of all task hours in model calculations.

(5) states that the total number of work hours expended in all task categories shall be equal to or greater than zero. This is a conventional nonnegativity condition required for linear programming computations.

(6) states that the proportion of routine task time performed by teachers in the division, less the proportion performed by paraprofessionals, shall be equal to or less than zero. This constraint has the effect of forcing a division of Rout task time between teachers and paraprofessionals when Rout time is a residual number of hours to be performed after teaching is accounted for in class hours.

(7) states the same kind of constraint as in (6), but in this case for OTH_t and OTH_a.

The model, therefore, takes into account the possibilities of a division of labor between teachers and their aides, and the solution will suggest the optimal hourly task mix for assignment of teachers and paraprofessionals that will fully implement the division of labor. The solution is principally dependent upon the magnitudes of the "a" and "c" coefficients. Given prior knowledge about the absolute magnitudes of these numbers (indicating that paraprofessional labor costs less and they perform more instruction per class hour), the solution for the model can be generally anticipated as follows:

Minimize NIN_t so that $NIN_t = K$, let Rout and Oth be done by paraprofessionals, and use all additional labor funds to introduce units of teaching done by paraprofessionals (NIN_a).

The Model Solution and the
Optimal Division of Labor

Results from the linear programming computations are reported in Table 7-1. The table is most easily interpreted as follows. The rows A, B, C, D, E from top to bottom of the table show the division of labor and changing hourly work assignments for teachers and their aides in the hypothetical school as the division proceeds in stages from no specialization of teacher (Row A) until final complete specialization of teacher (Row E). That is, the rows show the teacher and paraprofessionals' work assignments as teachers teach and do all other Rout and Oth (Row A), then as teachers teach and do one third of Rout and Oth (Row B), and so on down the rows until teachers only teach and are fully specialized professionals who do no Rout and Oth (Row E).

And down the rows, as teachers do less and less Rout and Oth in each row, their aides correspondingly do more Rout and Oth in each row. The paraprofessionals, therefore, are being introduced in greater number in the division as the rows successively show the division advancing from Row A to E.

The columns show the number of teachers and their aides, and the division of NIN, Rout, and Oth hours of work in the day, as the division progresses. For example, Column 1 indicates that teachers decline from 20 to 11+ and aides increase from 5 to 20+ (Column 5), as the division moves from no specialization

Table 7-1

Number of Teachers and Paraprofessionals Employed Daily in Hypothetical School and Their Hourly Work Production as the Division of Labor Progresses to Full Teacher Specialization in Instructional Tasks

Degree of Teacher Specialization	Professional Teachers				N of Para-professionals	Paraprofessional Aides			Total Daily Hours of $NIN_t + NIN_a$
	N of Teachers	Daily Hours of NIN_t	Daily Hours of $ROUT_t$	Daily Hours of OTH_t		Daily Hours of NIN_a	Daily Hours of $ROUT_a$	Daily Hours of OTH_a	
A Teachers do all daily ROUT and OTHER tasks (no specialization)	20.0	57.9	34.0	8.0	5.0	25.1	0.0	0.0	83.0
B Teachers do two thirds of daily ROUT and OTHER tasks	17.2	57.9	22.7	5.3	10.2	37.4	11.2	2.6	95.3
C Teachers do one half of daily ROUT and OTHER tasks	15.7	57.9	17.0	4.0	12.9	43.7	17.0	4.0	101.6
D Teachers do one third of daily ROUT and OTHER tasks	14.3	57.9	11.2	2.6	15.7	50.0	22.7	5.3	107.9
E Teachers do no daily ROUT and OTHER tasks (full specialization)	11.5	57.9	0.0	0.0	20.8	62.2	34.0	8.0	120.1

of teachers (Row A) to full specialization of teachers (Row E). Column 2 indicates that teachers always teach 57.9 NIN_t regardless of the stage of specialization. Column 6 shows that paraprofessionals teach a number of hours that increase from 25.1 to 62.2 hours daily as greater numbers of them are introduced (Column 5).

All data in the table, of course, represent the situation in the hypothetical school identified previously. Row A defines the initial school situation where 20 teachers are employed, 5 paraprofessionals are employed at a 1-4 ratio with the 20 teachers, and the total hours worked in the school day are 125 by all staff. Therefore, the complete table shows the change in the numbers of teachers and their aides and their hours worked in the day, as the division proceeds by stages from Row A to Row E. These points of particular importance are revealed by the results.

First, as teacher specialization is implemented in the division, the total hours of NIN_t + NIN_a (Column 9) increase substantially. This is the effect of the objective function where the function specified MAX NIN_t + NIN_a. Column 9 shows that total NIN is 83 hours when teachers are not specialized and their aides only instruct (Row A). But when teachers are fully specialized and paraprofessionals do all remaining Rout and Oth activities (Row E), total NIN rises to 120 hours daily for all staff. It is notable that all the increase in NIN is attributable to employment of increasing numbers of paraprofessionals.

Second, the results in Column 1 indicate that the numbers of teachers employed decline from 20 to 11+ as specialization advances. The number of paraprofessionals employed increases from 5 to 20+ (Column 5). As was anticipated, the model substitutes paraprofessionals for teachers chiefly because their labor costs less per hour than that of teachers and because they perform more NIN per hour than teachers. The implications of this substitution of paraprofessionals for teachers will be considered subsequently.

Third, the results in Columns 3 and 4 show the decline in teacher hours committed to Rout and Oth as paraprofessionals are employed to absorb teacher nonprofessional tasks. Paraprofessionals Rout and Oth tasks correspondingly increase as in Columns 7 and 8 as the division of labor advances. Note that in each row as the division advances, a total of 34 hours of Rout and 8 hours of Oth are always performed in the division. Paraprofessionals finally assume all hours of Rout and Oth when the teacher is finally fully specialized (Row E). The hours of Rout and Oth are always maintained at 34 and 8 because the work study showed that those hours of Rout and Oth may be necessary to support instruction in the class day. By definition, then, when the division is complete, the nonprofessionals assume all these nonprofessional activities.

Fourth, it should be pointed out again, for the table does not show it directly, that in all stages of specialization, A through E, the total daily labor costs for staff are $915.25. This is the budget constraint, that in the calculations in combination with the p and a coefficients, causes the task hours to substitute in the division, with the result that N teachers and their aides are determined for each stage A to E.

Fifth, and finally, the optimal solution for the objective function and for this hypothetical school is indicated in Row E. In that bottom row, teachers are fully specialized and none of their more expensive salary hours are committed to nonprofessional activities. NIN in total is maximized and rises to 120 hours as paraprofessionals are added to the division. Paraprofessionals perform all nonprofessional activities as they also add substantial instruction hours to the school day. And this result is achieved without exceeding the budget constraint of $915.25 for total daily labor. The model result suggests that efficiency can be obtained in the teaching division of labor if the solution is fully implemented.

Implications and Limitations
of the Model

Efficiencies can be obtained if the model is implemented, but undoubtedly nonspecialist readers will have some questions about the "realism" or the practical efficacy of the model. It would be surprising, for example, if some readers did not object because the model substitutes units of paraprofessional and teacher labor with the apparent assumption that these units are of equal quality or worth. The objection could legitimately be raised that substitution of paraprofessional labor for teacher labor may dilute the quality of instruction children receive.

Many discussions were held with teachers and administrators in the district schools to get informed views concerning the relative quality of teacher and paraprofessional instruction. As is true with so many qualitative questions, no precise answer could be obtained concerning the relative quality of teacher and paraprofessional instruction. However, few observers believed paraprofessional instruction was markedly different, in terms of its effects upon children, in comparison to teacher instruction. All observers were sure some paraprofessionals were superior instructors in comparison with some teachers. The author's own opinion, based on many hours of direct class observation, is that the quality of paraprofessional instruction was only moderately inferior to teacher instruction, in general, and the quality was almost on a par with teacher instruction when paraprofessionals were used to reinforce topics that teachers introduced.

Because no objective measurements of quality differences could be obtained, the following weighting scheme was devised as an approach to the problem. Assume that an observer believes, for any reason whatever, that an hour of paraprofessional instruction (NIN_a) is worth only 60 percent of an hour of teacher instruction (NIN_t). Precisely what the observer means when he says that a paraprofessional hour is "worth" 60 percent is not important. He might mean he believes children would learn only 60 percent as much, or whatever.

The total hours of NIN produced at the optimum in the division, which is 120.1 hours, can receive a penalty weight for the 60 percent estimate. For example, if the observer chooses 60 percent and the 120.1 hours at optimum consisted of 57.9 NIN_t and 62.2 NIN_a, then the weight of the hours is 57.9 + 60 percent of 62.2 and the result is a total of 95.2 total NIN hours. The 120.1 hours then have been negatively weighted for the observer's 60 percent disposition.

Table 7-2 shows this kind of weighting scheme for the 120 optimal hours when the negative weights are 60, 70, 80, and 90 percent. At 100 percent, of course, the observer would be indicating he believes that aide NIN_a is equal in worth to teacher NIN_t. There are some interesting generalizations that emerge from the results of the weighting.

First, it is notable that even if the negative weight is 60 percent, the total NIN hours produced per day in the school are 95.2, which considerably exceeds the 57.9 hours that teachers working alone produce. Put another way, even with a 60 percent negative weight, the 120 hour optimal production would only decline from 120 to 95.2. A generalization, therefore, is that the total hourly value of NIN does not decline precipitously, even if the value of paraprofessional instruction is estimated very low. It is true that the weighting scheme is somewhat awkward where it does not define the weighting basis. But it provides a demonstration that there is considerable latitude for negative weighting of paraprofessional hours, and the division of labor maintains a considerable output advantage even when substantial inferiority of paraprofessional teaching is assumed.

One other implication of the division of labor the table of results does not reveal directly is worth pointing out. It can be shown that if paraprofessional NIN_a is weighted as worth 50 percent of teacher teaching hours (50 percent of 57.9) in a day, that it will not be economical to hire paraprofessionals for any teaching. In those circumstances, paraprofessionals would be hired only to perform Rout and Oth tasks in order to free teachers to teach.

This point will first be expressed in terms of symbolic notation and then explained. Consider that if paraprofessional teaching hours are only as valuable as 50 percent of teacher 57.9 hours of NIN_t, then:

$$p_2 = \tfrac{1}{2} p_1$$
$$c_2 = \tfrac{1}{2} c_1$$

The expressions state that if paraprofessional teaching time produced in a day is equal to one half of teacher teaching time, then the cost of the paraprofessional teaching time is equivalent to one half the cost of teacher teaching time. What has been determined, therefore, is the limiting weighting case for substituting paraprofessional instruction for teacher instruction at their relative labor costs.

Table 7-2
Total Hours of Staff Instructional Time when Teacher is Fully Specialized and Paraprofessional Instruction Time Is Negatively Weighted for Hypothetical Quality Adjustment

Daily Hours of NIN_t at Full Teacher Specialization	Daily Hours of NIN_a at Full Teacher Specialization	Total Daily Hours of Staff NIN at Full Teacher Specialization	Percent Quality Weight for Daily Hours of NIN_a	Total Daily Staff Hours of NIN when NIN_a Percent Weight Is Added to Daily NIN_t (57.9 + %)
57.9	62.2	120.1	60% NIN_a = 37.3	95.2
57.9	62.2	120.1	70% NIN_a = 43.6	101.5
57.9	62.2	120.1	80% NIN_a = 49.8	107.7
57.9	62.2	120.1	90% NIN_a = 56.0	113.9
57.9	62.2	120.1	100% NIN_a = 62.2	120.1

Consider:

(1) paraprofessional hours of instruction are worth .50 of teacher hours;
(2) teacher hours of instruction are 57.9 hours;
(3) paraprofessional hours of instruction are 57.9 hours, but these hours are only worth 28.95, which is 50 percent of teacher hours;
(4) the cost of 57.9 paraprofessional hours at $4.29 per hour is $248.38;
(5) the cost of teacher hours at $8.08 X 57.9 is $467.83;
(6) one half of the cost of teacher hours is $236.91;
(7) then the cost of the 28.95 paraprofessional hours exceeds .50 of teacher hours because $248.38 > $236.91.

Therefore, the cost per hour of paraprofessional instruction exceeds the cost per hour of teacher instruction when paraprofessional instruction hours are weighted at 50 percent of 57.9 teacher hours. The decision would be to use only teachers for instruction if paraprofessional hours were so weighted in value, because NIN_t of professionals would be cheaper in obtainable time units than nonprofessional NIN_a.

Another potential limitation to the model solution is that paraprofessional labor is substituted for labor of professional teachers. Teachers and their professional associations might well find this implication objectionable. A first point to be made concerning this potential limitation is that the model could be altered to illustrate more or less paraprofessional substitution. Constraints could be added to reduce substitution.

The facts are, however, that whenever paraprofessionals are actually employed in real institutions, substitution against teacher labor takes place because paraprofessionals perform work professional staff would otherwise perform. The model only provides an illustration that makes this substitution explicit in an efficiency context. The extent to which anything like the model solution could be implemented might well be influenced by discussions between school administrators and employee representatives.

Another important question is the query, could the new mix of teacher and paraprofessional tasks be implemented in a school class scheduling plan? Is it realistic to believe that operations could be changed so that teachers would largely perform as teaching specialists? What would be the consequences for conventional staff roles?

Our own discussions with many teachers indicate that they are less than satisfied with the amount of nonprofessional work in their conventional roles and many would welcome opportunities to specialize in instructional tasks. "Resistance to change," therefore, would not appear to be a major problem. What would appear most useful would be school staff schedules that experiment with assignment plans that place nonprofessionals in classrooms as "homeroom" assigned staff while teachers become fully specialized professionals who visit classes during the day to teach. Such assignment plans would permit nonprofessionals to perform most of the routine work that housekeeping and child monitoring entails. Teachers, for their part, could concentrate on instruction as their duties were divorced from routine work. Schedules to accomplish these results would not be overly complex to devise, and they could be designed to maximize staff instructional contributions for given labor budgets.

The model presented in this chapter is the first quantitative model of the school division of labor that has been developed using real observations for variables. It is an illustrative model; and it is not the last word, in prescriptive terms, for design considerations for the emerging division of labor in the schools. The model was designed to arrive at a solution for complete teacher specialization in order to suggest the full range of potential cost, input, and output results that could result if specialization were pressed to conclusion.

Very often the value of intelligence gained from operations research is that it suggests general standards and principles that are worth identifying even if the real world limits full implementation of results and implications. Decisionmakers in many school settings are experimenting with new models for the instructional division of labor. The model has the very minimum value that it suggests that efficiency consequences of new arrangements be considered explicitly, and it identifies dimensions of work and costs that are relevant for consideration.

In terms of implications for the general cost effectiveness study, the model results amplify the conclusion, drawn from the work study results, that potential advantages of labor cost minimization and increased instructional output were not fully exploited in Portland because teacher specialization was not actually achieved. The model results strongly suggest that these advantages could be realized by effectuating specialization, along the lines discussed, in real and not model institutions. The actual magnitudes of these benefits, of course, could be determined only by practical experiments.

This chapter completes the reporting of study analyses that are concerned with the labor cost and work consequences of amendments to the teaching division of labor. A more general objective of the cost effectiveness study is to relate the costs of teaming teachers and paraprofessionals to the educational benefits their employment may have produced in the compensatory educational program in Portland. The following chapter identifies reading achievement gains that minority disadvantaged children experienced when they were instructed by teacher-paraprofessional teams in the district program for compensatory education.

8

Educational Benefits of the Compensatory Program

The primary goal of programs for compensatory education financed by federal, state, and local governments has been to reduce the disparity in educational achievement that commonly exists between minority and other children in school districts. In Portland, in years before the compensatory program was initiated, average reading achievement test scores of minority elementary school children placed them from one to two years behind the average achievement grade levels of white children in the community.

Analyses in previous chapters provided estimates of the instructional work and employment cost consequences of teacher and paraprofessional teaming in the compensatory program. This chapter reports results of an analysis of educational benefits obtained by the program. In this analysis, the reading achievement scores of children in the program were compared with scores of all other district children in similar grades to determine if program efforts reduced the achievement gap during the several years from 1965 to 1970.

Preliminaries to the Test Analysis Report

Chapter 2 discussed design considerations for the test score analysis in some detail. Here, points from that discussion that bear amplification will be noted. It is important to stress, first, that the measure of program benefits obtained by the test score analysis must stand as a minimum estimate of educational benefits of the program. In Portland, as in most compensatory programs, the emphasis was primarily to improve children's achievement in reading and language skills. For this reason, the analysis of reading achievement scores is a most relevant evaluation activity. However, nothing in the analysis will account for other benefits that children and staff experienced as a result of the program and the introduction of staff team instruction in program schools.

Our observations in the schools confirm the view that the welfare of school participants was improved in numerous ways because adult staff was increased as much as one half when paraprofessionals were present in ghetto schools. Behavioral problems received more attention, closer staff-child bonds were established, and similar difficult-to-measure but positive outcomes were fostered. Measurement resources were not adequate to account for outcomes of this kind. Consequently, an appropriate orientation is to consider the test analysis results as a minimum appraisal of total benefits. Moreover, the test scores themselves must be considered to be proxy measures of educational attainments.

103

Use of test scores for benefit measurement is not without special problems that often arise because of data limitations or difficulties that occur in adapting preferred research designs to particulars of an environment. Some critics have considered that measurement problems are so typical of compensatory education evaluations that they cast doubt on most evaluation results that have been reported in recent years.[1] The principal criticisms of evaluations are that control groups are inadequate, allowances are not made for effects of turnover among student populations, and longitudinal measurement of results are neglected. In this analysis, we went to some lengths to overcome deficiencies of these kinds.

Because all the disadvantaged children in the compensatory program received some instruction from teachers and paraprofessionals, it was impossible to establish control groups not instructed by teams. Fortunately, test results were available for the entire district third grade populations for all the years 1965 to 1970. The test used in those years was the McMenemy test for reading achievement, a carefully designed test suitable for research purposes. With this data, scores of program children and scores of all other district children in like grades could be compared for trend, with the comparison serving as a rather comprehensive control standard. The availability of annual test results for 1965 to 1970 also permitted annual score reviews as a method of longitudinal analysis. Longitudinal analysis was also achieved where it proved possible to obtain fifth grade test results for program students who were tested in 1970 who had been tested earlier in third grade in 1968. By comparing 1970 fifth grade and 1968 third grade reading scores, moreover, it was possible to determine how group scores shifted when allowance was made for student turnover in the program over the two-year period.

In what follows, third grade test results for program children are compared with results and trends of scores for other district third graders for the years 1965 to 1970. The special focus will be upon changes in scores of program children that occurred after the program was initiated; an improvement trend that reversed a trend of score decline in previous years, and a trend that ran counter to a general downward drift of all district scores during the period. In addition, the analysis examines longitudinal score shifts of 1970 fifth graders in the program, and appraises the impact of neighborhood and school population changes for program educational results.

Readers will want to bear these particulars in mind as the discussion proceeds: First, the analysis of third grade tests uses scores of all children in the district who were enrolled and tested in each of the years from 1965 to 1970. The scores are for tests that were administered once in the spring of each year to each third grade class. No data available permitted comparisons of two or more test scores for the same children in any year. Therefore, the analysis is not a study of test-retest results for identical children, except for the population of

[1] See, for example, Arthur Jensen, "How Much Can We Boost IQ and Scholastic Achievement?" *Harvard Educational Review* 39 (Winter 1969).

1970 fifth graders mentioned previously. The third grade score analysis evaluates scores of third grade populations for each of the years 1965 to 1970. In the third grade analysis, it was not possible to control for turnover of children in the populations because the annual test results include scores of children who entered the schools after annual instruction began in the fall of the year.

Second, the mean number of children tested in program schools in the six years was 550, a figure representing third grade enrollment in the eight to nine schools that were in the program over the period. The number of children tested annually in all other district third grades in the period averaged 4900 from 80 schools. During the years, the percentage of children tested of actual enrollment in program and other district schools was nearly 90 percent.

Third, the McMenemy scores used in the analysis do not have grade level equivalent scales that may be used to convert scores to an estimate of grade level performance of children. However, the all-district mean score levels were 50 on a standard score basis with a standard deviation of 10. This 50 average score level persisted for almost all the years with only a slight decline in the late 1960s. In the initial years of the program, the average for scores of program children was 41, almost one standard deviation below the average of the entire district population.

Finally, we now adopt the convention of identifying compensatory program schools as "AI" (Area I) schools and schools in the remainder of the district will be designated "D-I". Moreover, in the discussion a distinction will at times be made between AI schools with almost 100 percent black enrollment and AI schools where enrollment was shifting from white to black during the decade of the 60s. Test scores in the two groups of schools had different dimensions that are significant for the analysis. In discussion the first group of schools will be termed "stable black" schools, denoting persistent black enrollment. The other AI schools will be identified as "changing" schools.

Analyses of 1965-70 Third Grade
Reading Scores

The first reading achievement score analysis performed was a comparison of the mean reading scores of children in the compensatory program with the mean of scores of all other district third graders for the years 1965 through 1970. This longitudinal comparison was carried out first for several reasons. The analysis could show the trend of means of scores for both groups for years before and after the program was initiated. It was also necessary to establish basic facts about achievement performance of the district population, less the program children, which population was to serve as a control group for comparison with scores of program children.

Before the analysis, it was predicted that mean scores of program children would not shift upward, if at all, until at least the second year, 1967, after the compensatory program had been organized. This prediction was made because school staff indicated that the first program year had been devoted to organization, and not much exceptional instruction had been accomplished that year. In addition, our estimate was that results would not be strongly registered until a third grade class could be tested that had spent at least two of their three elementary school years in the special instructional environment.

The prediction was right in principle, if not exactly on the mark concerning the year when score gains were first measured by the achievement tests. Table 8-1 makes this evident. The information there shows that the mean of reading scores for all other district third graders varied over the six years by not much more than 1 score point, with a high just over 50 in 1965 and a low slightly under 49 in 1970. In the same years, the means of annual scores for children in the program show no trend of increase until 1968. In 1968, there occurred an upward shift of some three score points which was maintained with minor fluctuations from that year to 1970. The shift is moderate in magnitude, at least as indicated by mean figures, and is consistent after 1968.

The year 1968 is the first year third graders were tested who had experienced all their elementary education since first grade in the program. The observation of this improvement in scores after children were three years in the program may be a finding of no little significance. If these findings are interpreted to indicate that it may require three years for children to participate in programs and improve their achievement, then evaluation studies that review programs over one year periods may very well provide faulty appraisals of results.

For the specific purposes of this study, the conclusion from this first score inspection, subject to additional confirmation, is that there was sufficient improvement in reading performance by 1968 so that children in the compensatory program increased their mean scores by three points above their average scores prior to 1968. This means that the nine score point achievement disparity they suffered relative to all district children prior to 1968 was closed by about one third. A related finding is that the districtwide third grade achievement scores were sufficiently stable over the period 1965 to 1970 so that they could

Table 8-1
Mean Reading Test Scores of Third Grades in Area I and District Less Area I, 1965-70

	1965	1966	1967	1968	1969	1970
Area I score means	41.2	42.0	41.3	44.4	44.3	43.7
S.D.	10.6	10.4	10.6	9.7	10.5	10.1
District less area I						
score means	50.1	49.6	49.6	49.6	49.3	48.8
S.D.	9.7	10.2	10.1	9.7	10.3	10.7

serve as adequate comparison norms for appraising shifts in scores of program children.

Dispersion of Third Grade Scores 1965 to 1970

The inspection of annual mean scores provided little information about detailed distributions of reading scores in the years before and after the program commenced. The simple mean figures themselves are not very enlightening where they do not indicate where in the student populations improvement occurred. Closer inspection of the scoring distributions of clusters of children within the three point shift makes the composition of gains appear more significant.

To obtain detailed breakdowns of scores within score ranges, the following tabulations are made. The percentages of third graders in the compensatory program and in the remainder of the district that scored in the class intervals in Tables 8-2 and 8-3 were computed. The score class intervals show the percentages of children scoring above and below the mean score level of disadvantaged children for 1965, which was 41 points. Forty-one points is also one point over 40 which is one standard deviation below the all-district standard score mean of 50. The other class intervals of scores cover the complete range of scores in 10-score-point intervals.

As the intervals in Table 8-2 indicate, percentages of disadvantaged children in program schools shifted to higher intervals, especially in 1968 and years after. And as scores shifted upward, corresponding percentages of lower scorers declined because scorers were net scoring higher throughout the interval ranks. The year 1968 can be seen in detail to be the year of first significant change. In that year the percentage of children that scored in interval 41 and Over increased to 65 percent which was an increase over 1967 of 14 percent. The percentage of

Table 8-2
Percentages of Area I Third Grade Students Scoring in Test Score Class Intervals in Years 1965-70

Year	1965	1966	1967	1968	1969	1970
Class interval:						
51 and Over	20.38	22.29	20.80	28.62	32.77	29.36
50 and Under	79.62	77.72	79.20	71.38	67.24	70.64
41 and Over	53.66	54.49	51.10	65.02	63.36	63.30
40 and Under	46.34	45.51	48.91	34.98	36.74	36.70
61 and Over	3.50	3.37	2.37	3.71	6.25	5.28
51-60	16.88	18.91	18.43	24.91	26.52	24.08
41-50	33.28	32.21	30.29	36.40	30.49	33.95
31-40	29.14	31.09	30.66	25.97	27.27	25.92
30 and Under	17.20	14.42	18.25	9.01	9.47	10.78

108

Table 8-3
Percentages of District Less Area I Third Grade Students Scoring in Test Score Class Intervals in Years 1965-70

Year:	1965	1966	1967	1968	1969	1970
Class interval:						
51 and Over	54.08	51.86	51.53	50.90	53.16	50.81
50 and Under	45.92	48.14	48.47	49.10	46.84	49.19
41 and Over	82.94	81.05	80.57	81.31	79.03	78.94
40 and Under	17.06	18.95	19.43	18.69	20.97	21.06
61 and Over	12.08	13.24	12.97	11.47	16.29	15.30
51-60	42.00	38.62	38.56	39.43	36.87	35.52
41-50	28.86	29.19	29.04	30.41	25.86	28.13
31-40	12.88	13.96	14.03	13.97	15.18	13.90
30 and Under	4.17	5.00	5.40	4.72	5.79	7.17

children scoring in interval 40 and Under, of course, declined by a corresponding amount that year. The 14 percent improvement is about maintained in 1969 and 1970.

The 10-point class intervals in Table 8-2 that divide the score range permit more detailed identification of locations of upward shifts. The interval 61 and Over registers only moderate gains. Interval 51-60 shows there was a 6 to 8 percent increase in scorers after 1967 in comparison with earlier years. The same magnitude of declines is registered in the low-scoring interval 31-40 because students improved and moved up out of that interval in the same period. The interval 41-50 shows little net change and this is to be expected. If scorers are moving up within intervals from 31-40 to 41-50 to 51-60, the net effect on interval 41-50 would be almost no net change because scorers moving up into the interval would about balance scorers moving higher out of the interval.

The most significant shifts in score percentages occur from 1968 on in the lowest interval in the range, interval 30 and Under. As the table shows, between 14 and 18 percent of all children scored in this interval before 1968. But in 1968 and later, this percentage declined to 9 to 10 percent, representing a decline of nearly one half in the proportion of children in this bottom interval. Children who scored this low in the test range were very severely handicapped and would be almost entirely illiterate. They would also be most difficult to instruct in conventional educational programs. This reduction in the ranks of lowest scorers is a program achievement not to be slighted, and a most desirable outcome for a compensatory program. In general, the details of Table 8-2 demonstrate the information value of inspecting program scores as benefit indicators beyond simpler summary statistics.

The score results and interval summaries for D-I that are shown in Table 8-3 reveal the comparative stability of D-I third grade score distributions during

1965-1970. There is evidence of a very slight overall downward drift of scores in the period. However, the D-I score percentages do not change markedly and show no trend of overall increase as was experienced in AI schools. These score results for the general district give convincing indications that scores in program schools were improved by the compensatory program, even as D-I third grade scores showed no comparable trends.

Probability Tests of Third Grade
Score Distributions

None of the foregoing discussions of test scores employed statistical tests in arriving at judgments. To test the conclusion that program children made gains with probability tests, chi-square tests were computed to test significance of differences in the numbers of D-I and program children that scored in score class intervals 1965 to 1970. In these tests the hypothesis is that there is no difference between the two groups in terms of the numbers of children who scored in the score categories during the six years. Put in the affirmative, the hypothesis is that program children's scores differed significantly in their pattern from 1965 to 1970, especially where scores shifted to higher score categories during the six years.

Because slightly different numbers of children were enrolled in schools during the six years, it was necessary to adjust the data to insure that increases or decreases of scores in categories were not just attributable to changes in enrollment. For the six years, district records indicated that average third grade enrollment in the district was 5338 children, while enrollment for the program third grade averaged 613. These annual enrollment figures were then used to convert the percentages recorded in Table 8-2 into numbers of children. For example, the 613 mean enrollment figure for program children from 1965 to 1970 was divided by the actual percentage of children who in each year scored in each of the class intervals. The district mean enrollment figure 5338 was also used to convert the percentages for each year in the class intervals to "numbers" of children. Readers should bear in mind that the discussion will be referring to numbers of children that are reasonable proxies but not the literal number of children for any given year. However, the conversion procedure is not arbitrary in method or results. Actual percentages of children scoring in categories only have been adjusted by uniform annual base figures of 613 and 5338 in order to control for minor variations in annual enrollment and make the chi-square computation feasible.

The numbers of children scoring annually in the test score categories and the results of the chi-square tests are shown in Tables 8-4 and 8-5. Table 8-4 reports chi-square test results and tables for numbers of children scoring in intervals 51 and Over, 50 and Under, 41 and Over, and 40 and Under. These last tables were included because they represent D-I and AI mean score levels, respectively.

Table 8-4

Chi-Square Tables for Tests of the Null Hypothesis of No Differences Between Numbers of AI and D-I Children Scoring in Score Class Intervals, 1965-70

	Year	Numbers of Children AI	Numbers of Children D-I
Score class interval:			
51 and Over:	1965	125	2887
	1966	137	2769
	1967	128	2751
	1968	176	2718
	1969	201	2838
	1970	180	2713
	Chi-Square is: 32.519 (.001)		
	Degrees of freedom: 5		
50 and Under:	1965	488	2451
	1966	477	2570
	1967	486	2587
	1968	438	2621
	1969	412	2501
	1970	433	2626
	Chi-Square is: 12.730 (.05)		
	Degrees of freedom: 5		
41 and Over:	1965	329	4428
	1966	334	4327
	1967	313	4302
	1968	399	4341
	1969	388	4219
	1970	388	4214
	Chi-Square is: 21.598 (.001)		
	Degrees of freedom: 5		
40 and Under:	1965	284	910
	1966	279	1012
	1967	300	1037
	1968	215	998
	1969	225	1120
	1970	225	1125
	Chi-Square is: 40.054 (.001)		
	Degrees of freedom: 5		

Table 8-5
Chi-Square Tables for Tests of the Null Hypothesis of No Differences Between
Numbers of AI and D-I Children Scoring in Score Class Intervals, 1965-70

	Year	Numbers of Children AI	Numbers of Children D-I
Score class interval:			
61 and Over:	1965	21	645
	1966	21	707
	1967	15	693
	1968	23	613
	1969	38	870
	1970	32	817
	Chi-Square is: 7.076 (N.S.) Degrees of freedom: 5		
51-60	1965	104	2242
	1966	116	2062
	1967	113	2059
	1968	153	2105
	1969	163	1969
	1970	148	1896
	Chi-Square is: 32.126 (.001) Degrees of freedom: 5		
41-50	1965	204	1541
	1966	198	1558
	1967	186	1550
	1968	223	1623
	1969	187	1381
	1970	208	1502
	Chi-Square is: 2.717 (N.S.) Degrees of freedom: 5		
31-40	1965	179	688
	1966	191	745
	1967	188	749
	1968	159	746
	1969	167	810
	1970	159	742
	Chi-Square is: 7.822 (N.S.) Degrees of freedom: 5		
30 and Under:	1965	105	223
	1966	88	267
	1967	112	288

Table 8-5 (cont.)

Score class interval:	Year	Numbers of Children AI	Numbers of Children D-I
	1968	55	252
	1969	58	309
	1970	66	383
	Chi-Square is: 54.600 (.001) Degrees of freedom: 5		

The null hypothesis of no significance of differences between the numbers of D-I and AI children in the annual score distributions is rejected for all interval tables except the intervals 60 and Over, 41-50, and 31-40. These results indicate that numerous children in the compensatory program increased achievement scores relative to D-I children. This is a very conservative conclusion because the tables understate the number of improvers, especially in intervals 31-40 and 41-50.

This understatement occurs because in years when students improve scores, some student scores are registered in a higher interval while scores that might also have been in that interval, in turn, are shifted up into still the next highest interval. The net effect is that improvers entering the interval just balance those leaving the interval. That this effect happened can be seen by inspecting intervals 30 and Under and 31-40 for the years 1967 and 1968. The number of AI children declines from 112 to 55 between those years in interval 30 and Under. But the number of children in the next highest interval, 31-40, does not register those improvers who have moved up from the lower interval because there has also been a shift of scorers from interval 31-40 up to 41-50. The inflow of improvers from 30 and Under balances out the upward turnover. The chi-square test is not able to account for these dynamics of change which leaves so few apparent improvers in intervals between score levels 31 and 50.

However, while these dynamics mask the total changes the program stimulated, the statistical tests still record positive results for much of the change. In almost every subtable for the intervals, there are changes in the numbers of children in a direction of improvement—increasing in higher categories and declining in lower categories—1968 and the years after. Results of the analysis that are particularly worth noting are as follows:

Tests of categories 51 and Over and 50 and Under: From 1968 through later years, there was an increase of approximately 50 program children who scored in this higher category while, conversely, there was a decline of the same magnitude in lower scores below the 50 score level. In contrast, the number of scorers in the larger district is nearly stable during all the years. The chi-square tests are significant at 001. and .05 levels.

Tests of categories 41 and Over and 40 and Under: The score level 41 represents the mean score level of all program children before 1968. The chi-square tests for both categories, over and under 41, are significant. In 1968 and in later years, about 70 additional children score in the category 41 and Over. There is a decline of the same magnitude in the years 1968 and after in category 40 and Under. The numbers of children in the district annual columns are almost stable in all years.

Tests of categories 61 and Over through categories 30 and Under: In the total array of categories 61 and Over down through and including category 30 and Under, two of the chi-square tests for these five categories are significant: those for 51-60 and for 30 and Under. The numbers of children in category 61 and Over increases to show score improvement, especially after 1968, but at this high end of the distribution there are so few children that the upward shift is not significant by probability test.

In the two categories where results are significant by test, 51-60 and 30 and Under, the 1968 shift in numbers of improving children is very marked. In 51-60, the chi-square test is highly significant. The annual figures show that from 1965 to 1967, the mean number of children scoring in this category was about 110. But from 1968 to 1970, the mean number was in the 150s. In category 30 and Under the number of children in this lowest scoring category declined dramatically after 1967. There are approximately one half as many children in this category in 1968 and later years as there were in the period 1965 to 1967.

Children in this lowest category would be classified as mentally retarded in middle class school environments. Nevertheless, the program for compensatory education had its greatest impact in this category of most disadvantaged children.

The chi-square tests and tables, therefore, provide considerable detailed information supporting the conclusion that the compensatory program had influence on the scores of children throughout the score range. In particular, although the tables cannot be used to precisely enumerate actual numbers of children who improved, the data from both tables permit the conclusion that in 1968 and after in each test score interval from 20 to 50 percent more children scored in an interval 10 points higher than children did in years prior to 1968.

**Score Differences in Black Enrollment
and Changing Schools**

Three of the nine schools in the Portland compensatory program had almost entirely black student enrollment. Other program schools were located in neighborhoods where higher socioeconomic status white families were leaving the area and were being replaced by lower socioeconomic status black families. A result of these neighborhood changes was that several of the schools in the program were continuous recipients of children with objectively lower achieve-

ment potential during the 1960s. Table 8-6 identifies changes in these enrollment patterns from 1965 to 1970.

These enrollment patterns implied that some program schools might have
been especially handicapped in trying to improve programs and demonstrate
achievement gains in the 1965 to 1970 period. Especially if higher achievers
were replaced by lower achievers in all the program period, the compensatory
program would be so handicapped. Not only would low achievers replace higher
achievers but higher achievers would migrate with potential gains from the
program that would not subsequently be recorded on any achievement test
results.

The significance of the enrollment change factor was probed with chi-square
tests of the hypothesis that third grade children in the stable black schools and
the changing schools would differ significantly in relative achievement gains.
Tables 8-7 and 8-8 report results of the tests and the chi-square tables for each
score class interval test. For these tests, we were able to obtain figures for the
literal number of children in schools and verify that using actual numbers did
not bias the analyses. The tests are significant for score categories 50 and Under,
40 and Under, and 30 and Under. These are all categories below the district
mean scores. The conclusion is that there are significant differences between the
number of program children in black and changing enrollment schools who
scored in these categories over the six years.

Close inspection of the figures in the individual category tables reveals that
the number of children scoring in these categories declined as children improved
their achievement and moved to higher categories in 1968 and after. And this
improvement happened in both black and changing schools. However, in each of
the tables that have significant test results, a larger decline was registered in these

Table 8-6
Percentage of Black Enrollment in Nine AI Schools, 1965-70

	1965		1970	
School No.	Enrollment	Percentage Black	Enrollment	Percentage Black
1	941	96	616	93
2	352	92	338	85
3	1013	87	788	91
4	683	33	679	59
5	805	27	816	40
6	757	48	564	59
7	706	2	497	6
8	301	67	322	58
9	344	94	439	58

Table 8-7

Chi-Square Tables for Tests of the Null Hypothesis of No Differences Between Numbers of Black School Children and Changing School Children Scoring in Test Score Class Intervals, 1965-70

	Year	Number of Children Black Schools	Number of Children Changing Schools
Score class interval:			
51 and Over:	1965	21	107
	1966	25	94
	1967	26	88
	1968	35	127
	1969	52	121
	1970	33	101
	Chi-Square is: 8.6125 (N.S.) Degrees of freedom: 5		
50 and Under:	1965	245	255
	1966	162	253
	1967	182	252
	1968	189	215
	1969	150	205
	1970	125	210
	Chi-Square is: 17.0428 (.01) Degrees of freedom: 5		
41 and Over:	1965	116	221
	1966	84	207
	1967	85	195
	1968	114	254
	1969	111	223
	1970	87	211
	Chi-Square is: 3.6577 (N.S.) Degrees of freedom: 5		
40 and Under:	1965	150	141
	1966	103	140
	1967	123	145
	1968	110	88
	1969	91	103
	1970	71	100
	Chi-Square is: 12.3666 (.05) Degrees of freedom: 5		

Table 8-8
Chi-Square Tables for Tests of the Null Hypothesis of No Differences Between Numbers of Black School Children and Changing School Children Scoring in Test Score Class Intervals, 1965-70

	Year	Number of Children Black Schools	Number of Children Changing Schools
Score class interval:			
61 and over:	1965	2	20
	1966	1	17
	1967	2	11
	1968	0	21
	1969	8	25
	1970	5	19

Chi-Square is: 8.8829
Yates Chi-Square is: 5.6451 (N.S.)
Degrees of freedom: 5

	Year	Number of Children Black Schools	Number of Children Changing Schools
51-60	1965	19	87
	1966	24	77
	1967	24	77
	1968	35	106
	1969	44	96
	1970	28	82

Chi-Square is: 6.1086 (N.S.)
Degrees of freedom: 5

	Year	Number of Children Black Schools	Number of Children Changing Schools
41-50	1965	95	114
	1966	59	113
	1967	59	107
	1968	79	127
	1969	59	102
	1970	54	110

Chi-Square is: 8.2329 (N.S.)
Degrees of freedom: 5

	Year	Number of Children Black Schools	Number of Children Changing Schools
31-40	1965	88	95
	1966	74	92
	1967	78	90
	1968	81	66
	1969	62	82
	1970	55	68

Chi-Square is: 5.5292 (N.S.)
Degrees of freedom: 5

Table 8-8 (cont.)

Score class interval:		Number of Children Black Schools	Number of Children Changing Schools
30 and Under:	1965	62	46
	1966	29	48
	1967	45	55
	1968	29	22
	1969	29	21
	1970	16	32
	Chi-Square is: 15.1970 (.01) Degrees of freedom: 5		

lower score categories by children in black schools. In the table for category 50 and Under, the number of children in black schools declines from 245 to 125 between 1965 and 1970. The results in the tables for 40 and Under and 30 and Under are similar, with the greatest contrasts showing for the 1965 and the 1970 figures. The tables for the other score categories often show a 1968 to 1970 pattern of gains in higher categories and losses in lower score categories in both changing and black schools, but the differences are not so marked that they are statistically significant.

These results support the conclusion that stable black schools had more success in raising achievement scores than did changing schools, presumably because changing schools suffered from the dynamics of student turnover described earlier. One additional inference from the data supports this conclusion. Because of the white to black enrollment changes, it would be expected that changing schools would register losses among higher scoring children, at least in years before the program produced results. And because they experienced no white turnover, it would be expected that stable black schools would experience no decline of higher scoring children. Just this pattern of experience is revealed in the annual entries for numbers of children in the category tables of Tables 8-7 and 8-8.

The following experience with losses of higher scoring children can be identified for changing schools during 1965 to 1967:

Category 61 and Over with highest scorers declines from 20 to 11 children before turning up in 1968.
Category 51-60 declines from 87 to 77 before turning up in 1968.
Category 41-50 declines from 114 to 107 before turning up in 1968.

The magnitudes of the declines and reversals are not large, but the pattern of decline is consistent until 1968, the year of upward score shifts noted before.

In the same 1965 to 1967 period, the proportion of lower achieving children also increased slightly in changing schools:

Category 40 and Under increases from 141 to 145 before declining in 1968.
Category 30 and Under increases from 46 to 55 before declining in 1968.
Category 31-40 only decreases from 95 to 90, but it declines even more in 1968 and after.

None of the particular numbers for increases or decreases in these years is as important as the consistency of the trends: Between 1965 and 1968, changing schools experienced consistent losses of numbers of higher achievers and increases of lower achievers. In the same period, stable black schools experienced no consistent pattern of losses of higher or gains of lower achievers. All this information carries the key implication that changing schools were at an unusual disadvantage for purposes of obtaining achievement gains during years before and after the program. For most of the 1960s a downward qualitative shift in student body characteristics persisted. From the time the program was initiated, the compensatory program had to demonstrate results against this downward trend. In 1966, the program intercepted this trend, but it was not until 1968 that the trend was reversed.

Despite these circumstances, the score data indicate that many potential lower achievers in changing schools scored higher in 1968 and in years after. However, only approximately one half as many improved in comparison to numbers of improvers in stable black schools. These conclusions have important implications for the several analyses of third grade reading scores discussed earlier. All those analyses were carried out without controlling for differences in enrollment experience in changing and stable black schools. The reading score gains made in the schools can be considered that much more of an achievement because the evidence is that a majority of program schools had to arrest trends of ability decline before they could register gains in 1968 and later years. Would program results have been greater if the qualitative student ability decline did not exist to be intercepted? The results in the stable black schools, where there was no such decline, suggest an affirmative answer.

**Recapitulation of Results of Third
Grade Score Analyses**

The evidence of several analyses indicates that the compensatory program raised mean reading achievement scores from 41 to 44 by 1968 and later years. The program was in effect for three years before results showed conspicuously in 1968 achievement tests. The mean score shift from 41 to 44 narrowed a historical average score gap between compensatory program children and other district third graders from 41/50 in 1965 to 44/49 in 1970. More important, detailed analyses of the distribution of gains indicated that children at all ability levels improved scores, with a tendency for more lowest scoring children to improve. Only about one half of the historical number of children who usually scored in this low score position were still scoring there after 1968.

When achievement results for black and changing program schools were compared, results indicated greater proportions of children in stable black schools made achievement gains in some percentiles, especially in lower percentiles. Changing schools were under the handicap that the compensatory program had to intercept a trend of diminishing student quality in the 1960s. However, by 1968 this trend had been reversed and achievement scores in all schools were improved. This phenomenon of student quality trend and its reversal strongly suggests that overall scores would have been raised higher than from 41 to 44 average points if a majority of program schools had not encountered the trend of student quality decline.

None of the analyses discussed so far dealt with a very important question. This question pertains to achievement experiences of children who were enrolled in the program for their entire elementary grade experiences. None of the foregoing analyses controlled for student turnover in the program by focusing on such a continuously enrolled group.

Twenty percent is not too high an estimate of the annual student turnover these schools experienced, and it is probable that 30 to 50 percent of the children in third grades tested did not receive all their elementary education since first grade in the compensatory program.

The third grade data did not allow that children who had been enrolled in the program continuously from first grade could be identified. However, a complete set of 1970 fifth grade reading test scores was available for children who had also been tested in third grade in 1968. For these children, it was possible to compare results of their third and fifth grade tests and establish how well these continuously enrolled fifth graders maintained their earlier 1968 program achievement gains.

Longitudinal Analysis of Third to Fifth Grade Achievement Experience

The compensatory program in Portland provided children with special instruction from teacher and paraprofessional teams through fifth grade. In the third and fifth grade reading score analysis, the objective was to determine if 1970 fifth graders maintained, lost ground, or improved on levels of score achievement recorded in third grade in 1968. The availability of the fifth grade scores made it possible also to pursue other questions that the analysis of 1965 to 1970 third grade tests answered less than perfectly. With the fifth grade scores, it was possible to identify program children who had been enrolled in the program continuously from 1968 to 1970 and determine how their scores compared with scores of all of the 1970 fifth graders when this later group was not controlled for student turnover from the program.

In addition, the third and fifth grade score comparisons permitted closer scrutiny of the question about differential gains of children in stable black schools and changing schools in AI. By separating out children who had been continuously enrolled for the two years in each classification of schools, it was possible to determine if children in either changing or stable black schools made greater achievement gains.

The first question to be answered concerns the distribution of differences in scores children may have recorded between their 1968 third grade tests and their 1970 fifth grade tests. Did they gain, maintain, or regress in achievement levels? Table 8-9 brings information together that answers these questions. The columns in the table are arranged to show the third and fifth grade score differences of children who were and who were not continuously enrolled in the program between 1968 and 1970.

Focusing first on score intervals 40 and Over and 40 and Under, the data indicate that the percentages of children who scored in the 40 and Over interval declined substantially between 1968 third grade and 1970 fifth grade tests. This is true for both categories of children: those who were and those who were not continuously enrolled in the program. As the columns for both groups indicate, there was a decline of 10.4 percent of continuously enrolled children in category 40 and Over between third and fifth grade tests. The decline for children not continuously enrolled was 14.7 percent. Therefore, both groups did not maintain score levels achieved in 1968 third grade. The t statistics for the tests of significance of mean differences in proportions for the two years is significant for both groups.

The score class intervals, from 60 and Over down to and including the interval 30 and Under, provide detail on the distribution of score attrition between the two years for both groups. The mean difference columns are key information columns. They summarize the percentage declines of students in higher score intervals and the increasing percentages in lower score intervals between third and fifth grades. The continuously enrolled group experienced no statistically significant shifts in percentages of children scoring in intervals except for a 9.6 percent decline in the higher score interval 51-60, and an 11.7 percent increase in the lower score interval 31-40. The percent decline in this one higher score interval and the percent increase in the interval 31-40 are between them almost large enough to explain the net 10.4 percent decline of students recorded in the 40 and Over interval.

The pattern of declines for the total student group, not controlled for turnover, differs only from the pattern of the continuously enrolled group where the decline in percentages of students is one to two points greater in almost

Table 8-9

Percentages of Compensatory Program Children Scoring in Test Score Intervals of Third and Fifth Grade Tests, Comparison of Percentage Differences of Continuous Enrollment and Total Students

Test Score Class Interval	Percentage of Children in Class Interval 3rd Grade Test		Percentage of Children in Class Interval 5th Grade Test		Mean of Differences in Percent Between 3rd and 5th Grade Tests		t Statistic	t Statistic
	Continuous Students	Total Students	Continuous Students	Total Students	Continuous Students	Total Students	Continuous Students	Total Students
40 and Over	60.6	64.4	50.1	49.7	−10.4	−14.7	3.7 (.01)	5.8 (.001)
40 and Under	39.3	35.6	49.8	50.2	+10.4	+14.7	3.7 (.01)	5.8 (.001)
60 and Over	3.5	3.2	4.0	3.1	+ 0.5	0.0	0.3 (N.S.)	0.0 (N.S.)
51-60	20.7	24.9	11.1	13.3	− 9.6	−11.5	2.5 (.05)	3.8 (.01)
41-50	36.3	36.3	34.9	33.2	− 1.3	− 3.0	0.5 (N.S.)	1.4 (N.S.)
31-40	28.2	25.9	39.9	39.9	+11.7	+13.9	3.6 (.01)	5.1 (.001)
30 and Under	11.1	9.6	9.9	10.3	− 1.2	+ 0.7	0.3 (N.S.)	0.3 (N.S.)

every class interval. The *t* statistics are significant for the same intervals, moreover, at a higher level of significance.

The conclusion from this particular analysis, therefore, would be that there was a moderate decline of scores between 1968 third grade and 1970 fifth grade testing, the decline representing a net shift of almost 15 percent of scorers to score intervals below 40 score points. Even when the turnover of children during the two years is controlled by matching the test scores of continuously enrolled children, the net decline for this group was of the order of 10 percent of the students.

Third and Fifth Grade Score Differences for Stable Black and Changing Enrollment Schools

Close inspection of score data revealed an apparent difference between levels of test scores of fifth graders in black schools and in changing schools in the compensatory program. These apparent differences were tested in the following ways. First, *t* tests were computed for the mean of school score differences between results for third and fifth grade tests. The test scores used were those for the total of program children, with no control for turnover 1968 to 1970. These *t* tests of mean differences in scores were computed separately for the group of three stable black schools and for the changing schools. Results of the tests are indicated in Table 8-10.

The *t* statistic is not significant for the black enrollment schools, indicating that there is no significant difference between means of the test scores for black schools for the years 1968 and 1970. The entire fifth grade population of these schools, even when not controlled for turnover, maintained average score levels between third and fifth grades. The test results for changing schools are significant and the data indicate these schools had a mean score difference of −4.3 score points between third and fifth grades. The results of both tests make it clear that only changing schools, and not black schools, contributed to the general decline of third to fifth grade scores noted in earlier analyses.

This is a most interesting and unexpected finding. The third grade test

Table 8-10
Results of Tests of Differences Between Third and Fifth Grade Reading Test Scores, Three Stable Black Schools and Five Changing Schools

t Test Results, Black Schools		*t* Test Results, Changing Schools	
Differences of mean school scores between third and fifth tests:	−.762	Differences of mean school scores between third and fifth tests:	−4.34
t statistic: (N.S.)	.83	*t* statistic:	8.80 (.001)

analyses discussed earlier determined that the percentages of third grade improvers in black schools exceeded the percentages in changing schools from 1968 on. But both populations of students still registered net increases of higher scoring third grade students from 1968 through 1970. These later results indicate that the same pattern did not hold with older children who passed from third to fifth grades during 1968 to 1970. Only children in the predominantly black schools maintained third grade gain levels to 1970 fifth grades. And this means that the pattern of changing enrollments in changing schools was sufficiently disruptive to cause program results to diminish for fifth graders in changing schools, even while third graders in those same schools continued to make achievement gains.

Further corroboration of the pattern of third to fifth grade score findings comes from results of other analyses. In these analyses, t tests were computed for models identical in all respects with the models reported in Table 8-10, except that in this case the t tests were applied to means of school score differences for both school groups, when only continuously enrolled children's scores were matched and 1968 to 1970 differences in scores were computed. The result is that this analysis is identical to the earlier analysis, except that controls are introduced for student turnover in the period 1968-70.

As Table 8-11 reveals, the results of this analysis are much like the results of the analysis that used scores for total program students. Again, the t statistic is not significant for black schools, but the statistic for changing schools is significant. The magnitudes of the means of score differences for 1968-70 are reduced slightly as a result of comparing scores of continuously enrolled children and controlling for turnover.

Two more t tests give final, convincing corroboration to the findings so far described. In one of these tests, the third and fifth grade scores for all continuously enrolled children in AI schools were matched for each child, differences between paired scores were computed, and a t test was computed to test the significance of the mean of the score differences for the two tests. In a second test, the same procedure was followed, except that the scores of children

Table 8-11
Tests for Black and Changing School Mean of School Mean Differences Between Third and Fifth Grade Tests of Continuously Enrolled Children

School Category	Score Difference Between Mean of School Means for 3rd and 5th Tests	N of Schools Each Group	t Statistic	t Significance Level
Black schools	− .072	3	$t = .188$	(N.S.)
Changing schools	−3.642	5	$t = 3.97$	(.01)

who had been continually enrolled in black schools and in changing schools were separately tested. Results of these two tests are given in Tables 8-12 and 8-13.

The *t* statistic in Table 8-12 for the mean score differences for the complete population of continuously enrolled children is significant, and that mean of differences is measured as a decline of -1.8 score points between third and fifth grade tests. This indicates a very moderate decline of scores, but results for the second test are much more interesting.

Those results in Table 8-13 show that mean third and fifth grade score differences for continuously enrolled children in black schools and changing schools were very different. The mean score difference for children in black schools is a nonsignificant $-.08$, indicating no change in scores 1968 to 1970. But the same figure for children in changing schools is -3.1. These figures mean that all the decline in scores of all children who were continuously enrolled in the program from third to fifth grades is attributable to children in changing schools only. There was no deterioration of reading score levels for continuously enrolled children in stable black schools between third and fifth grades.

Cost Effectiveness Implications of Benefit Measurements

The results of the evaluation of reading achievement scores have singular implications for the cost effectiveness analysis objectives of this study. Because most fifth grade children in changing schools did not maintain their third grade achievement levels, the conclusion might be that the instructional program failed for most children who were enrolled from 1966 to 1970. A related conclusion might be that the new instruction produced by teacher-paraprofessional teaming was not effective, and that the additional resources expended for that instruction were wasted. But these conclusions would be erroneous.

It is more precisely accurate to conclude that the compensatory education program did not attain its objective of raising and maintaining achievement levels of most fifth grade children and probably most other children who matriculated to higher elementary grades. But there can be no simple inference from this fact

Table 8-12
Test of Significance of Mean of Third and Fifth Grade Score Differences of the Continuously Enrolled AI Students

Mean of differences 3rd and 5th scores:	-1.86
t statistic:	3.83 (.001)
Standard deviation:	7.42
N of students:	235

Table 8-13
Tests of Significance of Means of Third and Fifth Grade Score Differences of All Children Continuously Enrolled in Black and in Changing Schools

School Category	Mean Score Difference Between Student 3rd and 5th Tests	N of Children Each Group	t Statistic	t Significance Level
Black schools	− .085	94	$t = .109$	(N.S.)
Changing schools	−3.156	141	$t = 5.255$	(.001)

that the methods of compensatory education, in this case primarily teacher-para-professional teamed instruction, failed.

This would be an incorrect conclusion, first, because third grade achievement levels were increased enough for the entire student population to reduce the average achievement discrepancy by one third by 1968 and for later years. Second, third grade gains in scores were proportionately greater for the most disadvantaged children. Third, program methods actually reversed a downward drift of scores that had persisted in the 1960s. Finally, scores of children in primarily black enrollment schools with historically the worst achievement records did not decline between 1968 third grades and 1970 fifth grades. The partial population that did not maintain achievement gains was the majority population of 1970 fifth graders in changing schools.

The conclusion must be that the instructional methods of the compensatory program were relatively successful for student populations after 1968, except when program treatments were overwhelmed by changes in the learning environment that influenced educational opportunities of children in changing schools in the late 1960s. Program instructional methods, therefore, did not fail. By 1968 and after, these methods increased achievement of many students in lower grades, and did so against a trend of a downward achievement drift that was evident in the entire school district. Neighborhood population changes and their impact on schools, an influence independent of program methods, were responsible for the longitudinal decline in fifth grade scores that were measured. We should have liked to pursue the social system study that would have been required to identify the specific dimensions of change variables that were related to the decline in fifth grade scores. However, limited resources and the more specific mission of this study did not permit pursuit of the question.

If the purpose of this study was to perform cost effectiveness analysis of the compensatory program in general, and not analysis of the new division of teaching labor specifically, then mixed achievement benefit results like these would pose complicated analytical questions. Problems for analysis would arise in determining how to weight and associate program costs per child with program benefits that have mixed positive and negative dimensions according to the program years considered, the grade levels under review, and for black and changing school populations.

Moreover, because educators have not identified compensatory education program goals in specific, targetable dimensions, an analyst would encounter the problem of devising criteria to determine what degree of achievement gains is sufficient to justify costs of an entire program. Vague goals such as "reducing" or "eliminating" achievement differentials of disadvantaged children are usually the only "goals" specified. But, of course, because ability is differentially distributed in populations, the problem of goal definition is one of identifying relative shifts within populations that are feasible objectives.

The mission of this study, however, was not to arrive at comprehensive program evaluation. The objective was to evaluate the cost-effectiveness of the alternative method of instructional staffing: teacher and paraprofessional teaming. The test score analysis does not prove conclusively that the new instruction produced by teams was solely responsible for the achievement gains measured. However, considering that the new instruction was the principal program element that could have stimulated gains through direct instruction, the assumption of effects on student achievement is entirely warranted.

The results of the score analysis, therefore, indicate that the negative achievement differential was reduced by one-third for disadvantaged children when program efforts raised average scores three points after 1967. Qualifying information both adds and detracts from this summary statement of results. Children were enrolled in the program for three years, from first to third grades, before results were demonstrated. Program costs were incurred for this long before any effectiveness was demonstrated. Reflecting more positively on the program, however, are the facts that the program demonstrated most persistent gains for the most disadvantaged children, and did so against unfavorable qualitative enrollment trends and turnover.

The costs of obtaining these results were indicated in Chapter 6 and by the cost per ADM information reported in that chapter. For the years 1965 to 1970, the total annual incremental costs per ADM for the program were between $229 and $437. Incremental average costs per ADM of instruction, as a part of total average per ADM costs, were between $182 and $320 for the years 1965 to 1970. The per ADM costs of hiring nonprofessionals, as a part of average per ADM costs of instruction, were between $67 and $78 when highest levels of paraprofessional employment were reached in the years 1967 to 1970.

These three categories of per ADM cost figures, for total program costs, costs of instruction, and for paraprofessional costs, are all useful for purposes of evaluating the cost effectiveness of the teacher-paraprofessional instructional system. If one is inclined to believe that a school district, for whatever internal organizational reasons, probably could not organize and install a new staffing system without incurring exceptional costs as overhead inducements to innovation, then the higher total per ADM figures are probably the appropriate costs to consider.

Use of the annual average per ADM instructional cost figures might appear to have more merit where these annual costs reflect specific incremental costs for teacher and paraprofessional employment, the innovation that is most specifically of interest. However, use of this cost category for decisionmaking could not carry with it the implication that costs were expended for new staffing arrangements that were necessarily efficient. The work study data, in fact, indicated that the school district did not gain the teacher specialization that the instructional expenditures were intended to achieve. Of course, the result of the staffing innovation was production of more instruction per labor dollar spent, although this result was largely attained by paraprofessionals.

The average per ADM paraprofessional employment cost figures are of considerable interest where they indicate the comparatively minor costs, compared to teacher employment costs, of obtaining work and units of instruction from paraprofessionals. It would not be correct, nevertheless, to use these cost figures as primary data for cost effectiveness conclusions about the entire new work system. To do so would be to ignore that when paraprofessionals were hired, joint costs of teacher employment were also necessary because paraprofessionals could not have functioned without teacher guidance and assistance.

Our judgment is that the annual total per ADM cost figures for the years 1965 to 1970 are the appropriate figures to utilize for cost effectiveness evaluation. The conclusion, therefore, would be that when the district used the teacher-paraprofessional work system as an alternative to conventional teaching arrangements, the achievement gains realized by the new system were obtained at annual incremental costs per ADM that were between $230 and $430 in the program years.

Are there any existing standards by which one can judge if the expenditure of funds of these magnitudes to obtain results of this degree are somehow "worth it?" Nominal judgments of this kind would ultimately depend on individual value preferences for more or less expenditures to assist disadvantaged children. Whether society will pay the additional costs of new instructional systems in order to achieve learning gains of the levels that have been measured is, in the final analysis, a political question. For cost effectiveness evaluation purposes, the appropriate evaluation criterion is that which compares costs and outcomes under the new work system with experience under the conventional or other alternative work systems.

Finally, it should be noted that this study has developed cost effectiveness information and implications in addition to the conclusions that result from the achievement score and annual cost analysis. The analysis of hourly instructional costs in Chapter 6 showed that instruction could be produced at considerably reduced unit costs when teacher-paraprofessional teams were employed. And the linear programming analysis in Chapter 7 developed the implications that the new division of labor, if designed to achieve more complete specialization, might produce considerably more instruction while conforming to cost minimization principles. The total information in these several analyses clearly implies that programs to amend the conventional teaching division of labor could, at the least, have important cost minimization results.

9 Concluding Recommendations

This final chapter presents recommendations that result from study findings and our experience in performing the research. The principal recommendations pertain to school manpower staffing practices, public manpower programs for paraprofessionals, productivity measurement systems, and research for compensatory education.

**Recommendations for School
Staffing Practices**

The finding of this study that teachers produce so relatively little instruction, even when they are teamed with paraprofessionals, is a result that should prompt widespread experimentation with alternative staffing arrangements. Possibly some persons will dismiss these findings with defensive disclaimers that the results are somehow not representative or that emphasis on efficiency and work measurement is not appropriate to teaching as an art. But we doubt if many observers will review the findings and not conclude that teaching and learning opportunities are abundantly wasted under conventional teaching arrangements.

This appears to be the conclusion already arrived at by school administrators who have begun to attempt to rationalize the division of labor by employing paraprofessionals and by other means. The results from this investigation might appear to show that efforts to improve efficiency by employing teacher-paraprofessional teams have little effect as far as teacher performance is concerned. In general, this is what the data reveal, but we encountered few teachers who were not enthusiastic for the innovation. What we believe the study has established is that specialization of teacher work for more professional performance cannot proceed unless the traditional teacher work role is abolished and teachers are freed to instruct on a more full-time basis.

It seems certain this result could be achieved and the results proved in experiments in selected schools in a number of school districts. The general staffing model suggested for appraisal is one where paraprofessionals would assume the room assignments of teachers for purposes of performing the nonprofessional tasks that role demands. Teachers could then spend the greatest part of their time in direct instruction when they visited classes. To the extent that their duties permitted, paraprofessionals could join teachers in the periods of instruction scheduled.

129

There is no reason, moreover, why such a staffing system could not be operated at something very much like the total costs of instruction schools experience presently when teachers and limited numbers of paraprofessionals are employed in arrangements where teachers fail to achieve specialization. The essential problem of cost control in such a new plan would arise in connection with effective utilization of teachers. Scheduling experimentation of limited complexity should be able to establish more optimal teacher assignment patterns that would tend to maximize joint teacher-paraprofessional instruction while labor costs are minimized.

It is doubtful that districts would have to incur costs of instruction that would be as expensive as the Portland district experienced when teacher paraprofessional teams were employed. In that district, the incremental cost of employing paraprofessionals was a very small part of total costs of instruction. School districts that added only paraprofessionals to staff and did not incur the general overhead expenses of a compensatory program could experience costs much below those in the Portland district.

A final recommendation is that when districts find more basic staff innovations are impossible, they consider employment of paraprofessionals in much the same manner as they were used in the district studied. In these circumstances, the objective of achieving teacher specialization may have to be abandoned. But if managers are satisfied about qualitative aspects of paraprofessional performance, goals for increasing instruction opportunities at reduced costs should be attainable.

None of these recommendations for rationalizing staff work in schools can be considered so revolutionary as to be unattainable. Employment of paraprofessionals with teachers is no longer a completely novel practice and experimentation with the new division of labor is widespread. What remains is to rationalize processes in the new work division by considering more explicitly the efficiency consequences of work arrangements and objectives.

Recommendations for Manpower Programs

The study results concerning the work of paraprofessionals have implications for national manpower programs to employ paraprofessionals. The author has not been among the group of uncritical advocates that have promoted legislation for new careers for the unemployed in nonprofessional jobs. Those advocates have too often ignored the relevance of economic influences that may be consequential for the potential success of such programs. However, the results of this study suggest that paraprofessionals can contribute valuable services to educational institutions at effective labor cost to labor service ratios.

The Portland paraprofessionals were relatively well educated, but almost 30 percent were minority persons with low-income backgrounds. It may not be difficult to identify many capable people who could work effectively in schools in nonprofessional roles and recruit them from among the relatively large numbers of unemployed persons in the low-income neighborhoods of schools. The paraprofessional job applicant-to-hire ratio in Portland was extremely large during all the years of the compensatory program. Labor market statistics for urban areas all over the nation suggest that the labor supply situation of Portland schools would not be unique.

In the introductory chapter of this report, it was noted that changes in the financial circumstances of school districts have led educational administrators to experiment with paraprofessional employment. These decisionmakers have been pressed to rationalize the economics of the school division of labor because of the influence of financial constraints. Administrators in many districts have discovered that large labor pools of less than professionally trained persons are available for paraprofessional employment. Policymakers who are concerned that publicly financed paraprofessionals' jobs may not eventually be retained under local funding may not appreciate that school employers already have incentives to employ paraprofessionals because of the labor cost advantages involved. Considerable information in this study implies that employment of disadvantaged persons in paraprofessional jobs might be promoted and result in substantial private and social benefits.

Recommendations for Work
Productivity Measurement

Employment in service occupations in public industries has increased substantially in recent years. With this growth in employment, new requirements have developed for knowledge about productivity and work rationalization in public employment. Measurement systems have not been developed extensively because conventional productivity measurement methods usually associate labor inputs with final product outputs, a practice most elusive of achievement in occupations where results of services of persons have defied measurement.

The work measurement system developed for this study is not a conventional productivity measurement method because it does not associate final outputs with measured unit work inputs. However, the utility the system has for illuminating facts about teaching work suggests that this system, and systems for other occupations, could contribute greatly to knowledge to stimulate efficiency in public employment. Advancement in work specialization in the division of labor is one of the primary processes by which industrial societies achieve labor efficiency. To cite one application, measurement systems like the one used in this research can provide valuable guides to developments in specialization. And experience in developing the method suggests that systems can be designed to be replicable and useful for many settings where occupations are located. If systems can be developed for public service occupations in which large numbers of persons are employed, the efficiency consequences could be substantial.

The specific recommendation is that agencies of the federal government that have the mission of stimulating effective government operations encourage development of measurement systems of this nature. An objective would be to originate a series of measurement systems for principal public occupations. Systems could be designed to acknowledge the special character of tasks in particular occupations and be replicable for measurement in many different institutions where those occupations are found. Federal efforts to encourage development of systems of this sort should receive encouragement also from nongovernmental associations of public managers and employees.

Recommendations for Compensatory
Education Research

The experience of performing this study has taught us a great deal about problems in educational measurement and has acquainted us with measurement practices that are common in evaluations of compensatory education. The comments that follow are not an effort to claim special importance for the methods used in this study. They represent an effort to transmit experience and indicate how seriously deficient we believe measurement methods in evaluations have been to date.

Reviews of program evaluations that have used test scores indicate that evaluations almost always have the following characteristics. First, the program period covered by the test scores used is almost always a year or less. Second, the statistics that summarize results most often are group mean scores and simple measures of score dispersion. Third, the score analyses are seldom performed in ways that control for the entrance and exit of children in programs and the potential results on scores of student turnover. Fourth, data are aggregated for large student populations with the result that little is revealed about influences of residential population changes or other social system influences on potential achievement of children.

We can demonstrate why we are uneasy with the practices noted above and with verdicts of program "failure" that result from some evaluations having these features by reference to results this study would have obtained if measurement methods had the following characteristics:

- If scores had been examined only for any of the single years from 1965 to 1970. Achievement gains would not have been identified because gains were appparent only in trends between two or more years.
- If scores had been examined only for the period 1965 to 1967 or for the period 1968 to 1970. Positive program results were registered only after

children had been in the program three years, and a focus on these program "start up" and "plateau" periods would not have identified achievement shifts.

• If only 1968 third grade scores and 1970 fifth grade scores had been analyzed with no attempt to identify the influences of turnover among program children. The result would have been an erroneous longitudinal judgment that earlier achievement levels of all third graders had declined by their fifth grade school year. This conclusion would be consistent with the finding relatively common in other studies that children in compensatory programs usually do not maintain achievement gains during later school years.

• If no analyses had been performed to examine the influences on scores of enrollment changes in schools. No conclusion would have emerged that population changes in school neighborhoods were associated with declining achievement of some students and that children in black schools with more stable enrollment were benefiting more from the program and maintaining achievement gains.

• Most important, if any one of the approaches used above had been used as the primary analysis method, the conclusion would have been that the compensatory program produced no improvement in score results. The erroneous conclusion would then have followed that the methods of compensatory education had failed.

Experience from this study, therefore, suggests that program evaluations may be unreliable unless they evaluate program results for several years, they focus on particular students who have attended programs continuously and they evaluate influences of changes in neighborhood social systems as these changes may affect achievement performance. Because we know that most major evaluation studies have not done these things, we have little confidence that conclusions that compensatory education has "failed" are based on adequate measurement evidence.

Our final comments and recommendations reflect our experiences in performing the economic evaluations in the study. The experience has changed our views about methods of evaluation research that can have the greatest potential for gaining useful knowledge for scholarly and policy purposes. We are sure that given the state of organizational relationships in the schools, it will be most useful to direct future research emphasis toward analysis of the efficiency of detailed school arrangements that produce instruction for children. Much more needs to be known about efficiency at the level of school-service producing systems before more comprehensive cost benefit studies and other appraisals are performed at the level of more general systems.

We are convinced there are only very weak relationships between incremental resource expenditures for education and the ways existing school arrangements transform money inputs into treatments for children. There is considerable evidence in this study to support this conclusion. The results of the teacher and paraprofessional work study indicated that money expenditures produced more instruction. The finding that achievement gains were realized when resources were expended for new paraprofessional instruction suggests the possibility that greater gains might have resulted if teachers had actually been given opportunities to work in changed roles. But the results indicated more conclusively that the division of labor in the schools is so badly organized and so much inhibits teacher instruction, that it cannot be assumed that incremental expenditures for instruction produce additional and improved teacher instructional treatments for children.

Instructional services are by far the most expensive component of education programs. And the amount and quality of instruction children receive are surely potentially the most important determinants of school program contributions to achievements of children. Having performed this study and learned what we have about instruction systems in schools, we are not surprised that investigations like the Coleman study have found insignificant relationships between resource expenditures, conventional modes of school organization, and student achievement. Why would one expect that substantial achievement gains would result from incremental expenditures when ineffective instructional modes are the principal school program mediators between money expenditures and potential achievement?

The resources expended for instruction in American public education systems are prodigious. It should be possible to learn what additional amendments can be made in the division of labor for instruction to promote more effective relationships between school expenditures and teaching and learning.

Appendixes

Appendix A: Work Study
Reliability Analyses

The reliability of the work study methods and observations was examined by the following procedures. During the course of the study, two observers were assigned to code the activities of identical subjects during the 9:00 A.M. to 2:30 P.M. day. This procedure was carried out for subjects during the pretest of methods and during the Portland study. The objective of the procedure was to determine the interobserver reliability of observations for identical subjects who were observed.

The total of subjects so observed was seven, each of them for a full day, during the 1968-69 Portland work study. Four of the subjects were paraprofessionals and three were teachers. The total 38.5 hours they were observed by two observers was 9.3 percent of the total 412.5 observation hours the study obtained for all staff. Therefore, almost 10 percent of the observation study effort was expended in the reliability studies.

The reliability statistic obtained from the observations of the dual observers is a figure for the percentage of time agreement observers registered for minutes of the day subjects expended in IN, ROUT, and NONL activities, respectively. That is, the two observers' coding sheets were examined and, first, it was determined how many minutes each had coded for the same activity categories for the same subject in the entire day. The results of this procedure indicated only the total of minutes observers coded for each activity category during the day. The results indicated nothing directly about the minute-by-minute agreement for particular categories that coders might have registered during the day.

To obtain figures for minute-by-minute category agreement during the coding day, coding sheets were examined and the actual number of minutes per day when observers agreed and simultaneously coded the same category were determined. In the tables that follow, two kinds of figures are presented for observer agreement about subject expenditure of category time. The term "detailed minutes agreement" will be used to distinguish the minute-by-minute observers' work category agreement from the figure for agreement about total subject minutes for the entire day.

Tables A-1, A-2, and A-3 report observer agreement for interobserver reliability coding categories IN, ROUT, and NONL. Reliability data were not obtained for the other minor categories observed (ADMIN, EVAL, etc.) because those categories represented a very small percentage of all daily time of subjects. The table for IN instructional time will be considered first.

The table shows that observers' percentage agreement for the seven subjects, for the daily minutes of IN observed, ranged from a high of 99.4 percent to a low of 77.7 percent. The percentage for most subjects is in the 90s, all in all, quite satisfactorily high. The data for "detailed agreement" indicate that

137

Table A-1

Observer Agreement for Reliability Coding, Percentage of Observed Minute Agreement, Work Study Category IN

Subject Observed	Observers' Daily Minutes IN Observed*	Observers' Percentage Agreement†	Observers' Detailed Minutes Agreement‡	Detailed Agreement as Percentage of Mean of Two Observers' Minutes§
Paraprofessional 1	155. 150.2	96.9	142.1	93
Paraprofessional 2	43.6 56.1	77.7	42.1	84
Paraprofessional 3	142.3 133.3	93.6	123.6	89
Paraprofessional 4	168. 169.	99.4	157.4	93
Teacher 1	123.5 116.2	94.	106.5	88
Teacher 2	116.6 112.5	96.4	90.3	78
Teacher 3	61. 54.5	89.3	48.5	84

*Observers' daily minutes of IN observed is the total daily minutes each observer coded IN for the same subject in 330-minute day.

†Observers' percent agreement is a result of dividing the observers' number of minutes, the smallest number into the larger number.

‡Observers' detailed minutes agreement is the number of minutes in 330-minute day they simultaneously coded for the same category IN.

§The percentage figures in this column were obtained by dividing detailed agreement minutes by the mean of observers' daily minutes of IN observed.

percentages for that basis of agreement are also rather high, being in the 80s and 90s, except for one subject's 78 percent. The overall results of the table, therefore, indicate observers were very substantially in agreement in their coding for the greatest proportion of minutes observed in the day.

The table for the ROUT work category provides information about coder agreement that is only slightly less satisfactory. The percentage agreement figures in the daily minutes observed column are all in the 80s and 90s with one exception at 75 percent. And the column of percentages for detailed agreement indicates that all agreement percents, except two, were in the 80 percent range.

The situation is otherwise for the data in the table for the NONL category. There is substantial variance among the entries in the percent agreement columns for both daily minutes agreement and for detailed agreement. Many of the percentages are under 50 percent agreement and some are as low as the 20th percentile of agreement. It is obvious that coders had substantially different agreement experience when they coded in this category. We are sure the causes of the problem are as follows.

Table A-2

Observer Agreement for Reliability Coding, Percentage of Observed Minute Agreement, Work Study Category ROUT

Subject Observed	Observers' Daily Minutes ROUT Observed*	Observers Percentage Agreement	Observers' Detailed Minutes Agreement	Detailed Agreement as Percentage of Mean of Two Observers' Minutes
Paraprofessional 1	113.6 120.	94.6	104.5	89
Paraprofessional 2	94. 107.2	87.6	87.2	86
Paraprofessional 3	77. 80.7	95.4	69.9	88
Paraprofessional 4	99. 96.6	97.5	86.	87
Teacher 1	109.6 82.4	75.1	66.7	69
Teacher 2	145.7 148.5	98.1	127.5	86
Teacher 3	170. 179.	94.9	135.7	77

*The same definitions apply to this heading and to all other column headings, as the definitions in the table for IN.

Throughout the coding observers had some difficulty coding the NONL category, first, because the category title did not name or refer to actual activities performed. "NONL" as a title is a vague reference term, even though the activities in the category were defined under coding definitions. Experience suggests this lack of concreteness in the category title gave coders problems. In addition, a bad choice was made where "student control" was defined as an activity under the Routine (ROUT) category and "discipline" was defined under the NONL category.

We know that about one half of the observers had considerable difficulty making decisions about the appropriate category for scoring student "control" and "discipline." Moreover, they had problems in distinguishing between staff activities for control and direction of children and actual discipline. However, it was only apparent that these problems were prevalent late in the study. Any researcher who undertakes to use the methods and instruments of this study will definitely want to resolve these ambiguities before commencing his research.

We do not believe the lack of observer agreement in the NONL category poses any serious problems for use of all the work study data for this study for several reasons. A most important reason is that NONL category time was a very small proportion of all daily 330-minute time expended by each subject. For the two teacher groups, with and without paraprofessionals, mean NONL time was 9.5 percent and 11.8 percent of all daily time, respectively. For paraprofessionals, the figure was an even lower 3.5 percent of daily time.

Table A-3

Observer Agreement for Reliability Coding, Percentage of Observed Minute Agreement, Work Study Category NONL

Subject Observed	Observers' Daily Minutes NONL Observed*	Observers' Percentage Agreement	Observers' Detailed Minutes Agreement	Detailed Agreement as Percentage of Mean of Two Observers' Minutes
Paraprofessional 1	7.5 16.	46.8	5.9	50
Paraprofessional 2	26.7 24.4	91.3	19.3	75
Paraprofessional 3	16. 18.6	86	11.7	67
Paraprofessional 4	12.5 15.6	80.1	10.1	72
Teacher 1	21.4 47.7	44.	16.5	47
Teacher 2	31.5 18.	57.1	13.9	56
Teacher 3	15.5 36.1	42.9	4.3	16

*The same definitions apply to this heading and to all other column headings, as the definitions in the table for IN.

More important, we have seen that IN and ROUT were coded very much in agreement by observers, and this study has relied on IN and ROUT observation time data most substantially in the inferences about work patterns, work differences of groups, and in the cost and linear programming discussions. And IN and ROUT times were a large proportion of all staff daily time expended in work. The summary data of the work study indicate teachers with and teachers without paraprofessionals expended 33.1 percent and 27.8 percent of daily time in IN, respectively. Their respective figures for ROUT were 38.5 percent and 43.5 percent. Paraprofessionals also spent a percentage of daily time for both IN and ROUT activities that was in the 30 percents.

It is clear, therefore, that in the activity categories that count quantitatively, observers had quite satisfactory interobserver agreement. One more source of information increases our confidence in the methods and their reliability. This is the result obtained in the second year sampling work study discussed in Appendix B.

Appendix B: Work Study
Methodological Appendix

This appendix provides more detail about subject selection, work study design, and related matters than methodological Chapter 2 reported. Researchers who anticipate adopting work study methods to their own uses will especially want to review the information in these pages. In succession, the topics considered are selection of subjects, schools and observation schedules, characteristics of subjects, and statistical analyses of subject work and personal characteristics.

Selection of Schools and Subjects

Before the field work was begun in Portland, extensive consideration was given to possible methods for sampling the work activities of subject population. One sampling plan would have been to define populations with stratification for schools, for grades in schools, for teachers and aides in grades, and for intervals during the day when work would be observed. More specifically, conceivable statistical control could be elaborated to obtain representativeness of institutions, grades, subjects, and the daily distribution of the work phenomena to be observed. The problems we encountered in efforts to meet such specifications were as follows.

A basic problem was that no information was available from any source that identified hypothetical universe dimensions for teacher and aide work. A sampling plan would require that some information be known about such universes so that empirical observation schedules could be planned in the light of universe characteristics. This problem and a more practical problem finally led us to adopt the plan of assigning observers to teachers and paraprofessionals for a full work day to gain observations.

That practical problem was that it proved impossible to implement any sampling plan that would assign observers to different schools, subjects, and classes during different hours of the school day. To do so meant that observers would have formidable logistical problems moving between subjects and classes even in any one school. Observers would also have to obtain acceptance from new subjects several times a day. More important, a study could not flood schools with outsiders who might disrupt classes and staff with constant comings and goings. This was an observation study. To have observers coming and going would have been unsettling for staff, to say the least.

Because of these limitations, a final decision was made to perform the study by assigning observers to teachers and paraprofessionals for the full school day when children were in school: from 9:00 A.M. to 2:30 P.M. Observers ultimately coded subjects' activities throughout the day, except for subject break and free time. The result is that the problem of determining a sampling frame for sampling subjects' activities was solved by the strong expedient of observing the work day comprehensively!

When the plan to observe subjects for full days was decided, we had some concern that this procedure might demand too much of observers' and subjects' tolerance for each other. In fact, observers proved to be up to the task and remarkable tolerance was experienced from subjects. In part, this tolerance developed because researchers were careful to arrange entry to the schools so that subjects understood we were independent researchers and no data would later be reported in association with subjects' identities.

We also made special trips to the schools on days before observations began and talked to all teachers and paraprofessionals in the school to inform them of our plans, purposes, and obtain their acceptance of the project. These efforts were worthwhile. Not once did a subject object to the presence of observers, and disruptions in classes were minimal.

The question naturally arises: Did not staff perform at their very best behavior because they knew they were being observed? Presumably they might have done so, but we were in the schools for a while, the staff got to know us, and relationships were not strained. If the reader chooses, he can consider that the observations were gained from subjects that were usually on their best behavior. The real facts, we suspect, are that staff did not have much time to be self-conscious about our presence. A room with some twenty-five children is a busy place.

The schools in the study were selected and not sampled because the primary study focus was not on all Portland schools but the limited number in the compensatory program for disadvantaged children. Most of the data for the study was obtained from the three schools in that program that had the largest minority enrollment. This selection of schools was made, first, because it proved impractical to visit multiple schools and facilitate entry and acceptance in the many schools that might "fall into" a sample. Second, for reasons of social relevance it was important to concentrate scarce research resources on schools serving the most disadvantaged children in the city. Third, by selecting schools with more "difficult" educational environments we believed the study would produce "conservative" estimates, indicating what teachers and their aides might (or might not) be able to accomplish under greater handicaps to effective pedagogy.

In addition to these three schools, five other schools were visited in the district that were outside the ghetto area and not in the compensatory program. These schools were in lower middle-class and middle-class neighborhoods. Teachers and aides in lower grades were observed in these schools to obtain comparison data to determine how nonprofessionals worked with teachers in more ordinary grade school environments. Also, because all teachers in Area I had paraprofessionals assigned to them, these other nonghetto schools were used as the source of the population of teachers-without-aides for this study. It should be noted at this point that statistical tests indicated that there was no significant difference between the work performed by the teachers with paraprofessionals in the nonghetto schools and the teachers with paraprofessionals in the three ghetto schools.

When the decision was made to concentrate study effort in the schools referred to above, a decision was also made to limit the study to grades one to four and observe all teachers and their paraprofessionals in those grades in the schools. The decision to observe all staff in the grades was made as an alternative to sampling because, again, we had no information about any hypothetical work parameters that could be used to design a staff-work sampling plan. The conservative solution to this dilemma that was decided upon, therefore, was to observe the "universe" of all staff in the schools chosen for study.

Grades one to four were chosen for study because (a) paraprofessional employment was concentrated in those grades, (b) we accepted the contemporary view that early learning years are the critical years that shape the educational experience of children, and (c) test data for purposes of measuring program benefits was more adequate for children in elementary grades in the district.

In summary, the work study was performed in 1968-69 in eight schools and with all teachers and paraprofessionals in grades one to four in those schools in two administrative areas of the district, Area I and Area II. The total of teachers observed for a full work day was twenty-seven teamed teachers and twenty teachers without paraprofessionals. Twenty-seven paraprofessionals who were assigned to the teachers were observed.

Obviously the study made compromises with canons of statistical theory where theory prescribes that sampling of subjects is desirable in research. Our principal problem was that we could not obtain acceptance for the study or perform the complicated logistics that would be required if a sampling plan had been used to identify schools and subjects randomly for observation. Nevertheless, we have information that indicates the selection methods we used probably did not cause the work phenomena observed to be substantially different from dimensions a random method of selection might have obtained.

In this context, consider that the final product of the observation study was observations describing the activities staff performed during school days. These observations were gained from subjects who worked in relatively similar class situations in a school district that had uniform rules for class scheduling, curricula, work expectations for teachers, and other organizational features. The teacher-pupil ratios were not very different in all schools. In schools in the compensatory program, the chief feature that differentiated those schools and classes was the presence of paraprofessionals—the difference we sought to observe.

The point is that under these circumstances of relative similarity of organizational setting, one might expect the chief differences in work activities of staff would derive from individual differences in the organization setting. Data available to us indicate that the teachers and the paraprofessionals in Area I and II were substantially similar in personal characteristics with other teacher and paraprofessional populations in the district.

Personal Characteristics of Subjects

A number of statistical tests were performed to determine if Area I and Area II teachers and paraprofessionals differed significantly in terms of personal and other characteristics. The objective of these procedures was to provide information to judge if the groups that were selected for study differed in significant ways from each other (Area I staff vs. Area II staff) or differed significantly from larger populations in the district. Before reporting results of these tests, characteristics of the subjects will be noted.

Table B-1 reports such information. In general, the data indicate that the

Table B-1
Characteristics of the Teacher and Paraprofessional Subjects Observed in the Work Study, 1968 Data

	Teachers with Paraprofessionals (N-27)	Teachers without Paraprofessionals (N-20)	Paraprofessionals (N-28)
Mean age	34.2	38.7	37.5
Number male	1	1	0
Number white	27	19	20
Number married	18	14	25
Mean years education	16.1	16.2	13.2
Months' teaching experience	60.	118.	16.3
Mean salary 1968-69	$7678.	$8007.	$4149.
Mean number students in classes	22.8	24.9	NA
Percentage minority students in classes	60.2	20.9	NA
Distribution of teachers by grade level	Grade 1: 7 Grade 2: 7 Grade 3: 8 Grade 4: 6	Grade 1: 5 Grade 2: 5 Grade 3: 6 Grade 4: 4	

teacher groups were substantially alike in terms of personal characteristics. There are moderate differences in age and a larger difference in teaching experience. This variable represents all months of teaching experience in careers.

In order to test for significance of differences between the two teacher groups, analyses of variance were computed to obtain F ratios for between and within group variance for the characteristics reported in the table. The F ratio for the age variable is 1.16 and is not significant at .01 where $F(1,45) = 7.26$.

F statistics were computed also for the variables sex, race, marital status, months teaching experience, 1968-69 salary, number of students in class, and percent of minority students in class. Only the tests for the variable months of teaching experience and percent of minority children were significant. The F for teaching experience is 5.3 which is significant at .05. The F ratio for percent of minority students is 20.0, which is significant at .01.

The conclusion from these tests is that teacher groups were not significantly different in terms of personal characteristics and class variables, except for teaching experience and class minorities. The finding that classes differed significantly in percentages of minority children is not surprising because of differences between Area I and Area II enrollment patterns. We conclude that the two teacher groups were not significantly different except for one variable. But is relative experience a variable related to classroom performance in a way that could cause differences in the work observations the study obtained for teachers?

No analysis performed answers this question directly. However, several analyses carried out indicate that the mean daily work category minutes of various subject groups were not related significantly to personal variables, including teaching experience. In one of these analyses, a regression equation was computed to examine association between the variables daily minutes of IN time observed and months of teaching experience for the twenty-seven teachers who worked conventionally.

The results for the equation indicate a correlation between the dependent variable IN and independent variable teaching experience of $-.22$, an intercept value of 29.7 and a regression coefficient of 1.040. The T and the F values are not significant. For these teachers, there is no significant relationship between teaching experience and the work variable IN. Close inspection of data for all subject groups leads us to conclude that none of the subject variables we could obtain data for have significant association with measured work category times.

The analyses reported above support the conclusion that the teachers teamed and not teamed with paraprofessionals did not differ in terms of characteristics that might be associated with differences in work results that were observed for the two groups. But results from analyses of variance studies indicate that the two groups did not differ significantly, in fact, in the amounts of time they expended daily in the work categories. In these analyses the group mean daily minutes expended in categories IN, ROUT, NONL, OUT, and OTHER were data entries for the analyses. Table B-2 reports the results.

Table B-2

Analyses of Variance of Mean Daily Work Category Minutes for the Teacher with Paraprofessional and the Teacher without Paraprofessional Subjects

Variable	IN	ROUT	NONL	OUT	OTHER
Teachers with paraprofessionals					
Mean minutes	109.28	127.27	31.64	47.91	13.87
S.D.	37.54	36.98	18.28	22.16	13.28
Teachers no paraprofessionals					
Mean minutes	92.04	143.69	38.93	49.88	5.44
S.D.	24.79	35.74	18.47	19.88	6.35
Total sample					
Mean minutes	101.94	134.25	34.74	48.75	10.29
S.D.	33.54	36.98	18.52	21.02	11.58
Between variance	3418.00	3099.00	610.79	44.34	816.71
Within variance	1074.11	1329.74	337.8	450.69	118.99
F ratio	3.18	2.33	1.81	0.09	6.86*

*Significant at .05

To be significant at .05 the F ratio for each of the five analyses would have to exceed 4.06. Only the F ratio for the activity category OTHER exceeds the 4.06 level and is significant. This is the least interesting and important of the activity categories because it is only a composite of the total of subjects' AIDE, EVAL, and PLAN observed times.

The more important conclusion is that the differences for the groups for IN and ROUT categories are not significant. The two teacher groups did not differ significantly in terms of their mean times that were recorded for each category for the total 330-minute day.

The teacher groups, then, were not significantly different in terms of personal characteristics and observed work category mean times. There remains to assess the evidence for the teachers who worked with paraprofessionals from Area I and Area II. Did our selection of these subjects by nonrandom means identify two subject groups that are distinctly different?

Analyses of variance were performed for the same personal characteristics, school variables, and work category variables as were analyzed for the two groups discussed previously. F statistics significant at .01 were obtained for the variables of the number of students in class and the percentage of minority students in class in these one-way analyses for the sixteen subjects in Area I and the eleven in Area II. (The results of the analyses are not shown by table.) In addition, an F statistic significant at .05 was registered for 1968-69 salary mean comparisons for the group. The Area I salary mean was $8222 and the Area II salary mean was $6886.

It is doubtful that these differences are associated with differences in work output. The analyses of variance of category mean times for IN, ROUT, and the other categories indicate that there are no significant differences in category times for the groups. The means for IN are 109.36 and 109.17. The means for ROUT are 124.69 and 131.02. The conclusion is that Area I and Area II teachers who worked with paraprofessionals were relatively homogeneous in terms of personal characteristics and their daily measured work.

A final analysis focused on paraprofessionals who were included in the study. In order to tabulate data on their personal characteristics, we drew a random sample of eighty personnel files from the total four-hundred paraprofessional files in the district personnel office. Then significance of differences of paraprofessional mean age and mean years of education were tested by t test for the twenty-eight paraprofessionals in the study and the eighty drawn randomly from the files. The comparative mean age and education figures for the two groups were 37.5/37.8 for age and 13.2/13.8 for years education. By these tests, which were not significantly different, the populations of paraprofessionals in our study and in the larger district were not significantly different in characteristics.

A 1969-70 Replication of the Work Study

The work study data reported in earlier chapters of this study were obtained at the schools in 1968-69. It was desirable to replicate this study in the second year of the research, 1969-70, for several reasons. First, we wanted to extend the longitudinal scope of the study and to be sure the work phenomena observed in 1968-69 were relatively stable dimensions of work that persisted in the district over time.

Second, additional data for a different year, where data were otained by the same instruments, would provide a check on the replicability of the work study. If results from the second year were substantially the same as results for the first year, this would increase confidence in the instruments, methods, and permanence of dimensions of work studied.

Third, we wanted in a repeat observation study to try to gain useful observations on a sampling basis. The data of the major study of 1968-69 were obtained by observing selected staff for a full day. We thought we had learned enough after that study to indicate that a more efficient sampling method might be employed where staff would be observed for much less than a full day. Details of the briefer 1969-70 observation study are as follows.

The study was carried out only in the three Area I schools with the greatest proportion of black student enrollment. Again we concentrated on three schools because it was not practicable to make arrangements for sampling schools. In those schools, the research staff spent only one hour of the day observing each teacher and paraprofessional in grades one through four. Furthermore, the total clock hours observed were sampled so they were approximately equally distributed across all work hours of the day.

Eighteen teachers and fourteen paraprofessionals, therefore, were each observed for one hour in the day where total hours for observation were spread between 9:00 A.M. and 2:30 P.M. The total observation hours accordingly were 14 plus 18, or 32 hours in total. We were not able to distribute the hours exactly equally between 9:00 A.M. to 2:30 P.M., but the distribution of hours over the day, except for lunch hours, was approximately equal.

The expectation, therefore, was that this second study might provide observation data for work categories that would indicate teachers and their aides spent the same proportion of time in IN, ROUT, and other categories, even though the time period was one year later and the observation duration was one hour, not one day per subject.

Tables B-3 and B-4 bring together summaries of data from the second work study and make comparisons with data from the more extensive study of 1968-69. The tables for teachers and for paraprofessionals show the category

Table B-3

Comparison of 1968-69 and 1969-70 Work Study Results, Percentages of Work Category Time Observed for Teacher with Paraprofessional Subjects

Work Category	Percentages for 1968-69 Teachers	Percentages for 1969-70 Teachers
IN	33.1	37.5
ROUT	38.6	39.5
NONL	9.6	13.9
OTHER	4.2	6.6
OUT	14.5	2.5
	100.0%	100.%

Table B-4

Comparison of 1968-69 and 1969-70 Work Study Results, Percentages of Category Time Observed for Paraprofessional Subjects

Work Category	Percentages for 1968-69 Paraprofessionals	Percentages for 1969-70 Paraprofessionals
IN	39.0	36.2
ROUT	35.8	31.7
NONL	3.6	11.1
OTHER	6.8	7.6
OUT	14.8	13.4
	100.0%	100.0%

times, as a percentage of total day activities, that were obtained in the more extensive 1968-69 study and the results from the 1969-70 study. The percentages in the columns for the 1968-69 group are the mean percentages of time spent in each work category during 330-minute days. The percentages for the 1969-70 group observed are group mean percentages of time spent in each category where each subject was observed for one hour during the teaching day.

The data for teachers indicate the second study replicated results of the 1968-69 study with very similar category times despite the large differences in time spent with subjects. The IN and ROUT categories are very comparable, and only the OUT category is substantially different in the two studies. This difference in the OUT percentages is almost entirely explained because observers did not observe during noon hours.

The category times for paraprofessionals in their table show the same comparability between the two studies. Only the NONL category is much at variance between the two studies. Again, these categories that occupy most of the staff time, IN and ROUT, are quite similar. The lack of comparability in the NONL category can be attributed to problems that new observers in the second study had in distinguishing between the student "control" and "discipline" factors in the ROUT and the NONL categories.

Considering the enormous differences in total hours of subject observation time that characterize the two studies, the results of the second study are quite satisfactory. The 1969-70 results obtained by observing subjects for only one hour in the day indicate it is possible, on this sampling basis, to replicate the larger study that observed subjects for an entire day. The results lend credibility to the method and the instruments used. The results also indicate that the dimensions of work observed are relatively stable dimensions of teacher and paraprofessional activity, at least in Portland under the forms of school organization that existed during recent years.

About the Author

Eaton H. Conant is a Professor at the College of Business Administration, University of Oregon, and Director of the Industrial Relations Institute at that university.